INDIA ∝ MOROCCO ∝ SYRIA

FEAST BAZAAR

BARRY VÉRA

MURDOCH BOOKS

CONTENTS

'A loaf of bread,' the Walrus said,
'Is chiefly what we need:
Pepper and vinegar besides
Are very good indeed—
Now if you're ready, Oysters dear,
We can begin to feed.'

Lewis Carroll, *Through the Looking-Glass*

Have you ever wondered why we eat the food we do? Where the food customs we take for granted actually began? I mean, who decided to eat snails and how did this obscure mollusc become such a delicacy? And once you're thinking about snails, you might wonder what kind are used, and how they are bred. As a chef, I have always wondered about the food I cook, and how each recipe I use became a recipe.

For me, the journeys I have taken while filming the television programs *Feast India* and *Feast Bazaar* have given me the opportunity to explore the rich cultures of India, Morocco and Syria and have some of these questions answered. I delved deeply into the culinary history of each country and explored the rituals that surround the preparation, cooking and eating of regional foods as I went.

India was our first destination and appealed to me because it has so much to offer in its culinary pot—the food is so different to what we are used to eating, traditionally, in the Western world. A curry is not just about being hot; it's about creating a dish in such a way as to be able to taste the individual spices in every mouthful. Travelling through India made me consider particular ingredients on a new level. For example, in the West we tend to use salt and pepper without having any knowledge of their origins, the history behind them or the wars that have been fought in their name. After learning about black pepper in the Spice Mountains of the Western Ghats and the salt mines of Rajasthan, I had a new respect for these two key ingredients and the way they are used.

Visiting Morocco brought new insights into the bazaars and souks of the Islamic world—from the windblown coast of Essaouira and the mystique of the square in Marrakech to the incredible scenery of the High Atlas Mountains and the labyrinth of streets in Fez.

Syria has more history than I could ever have imagined—from Damascus, which is said to be the oldest inhabited city in the world, to the ancient city of Aleppo, my eyes were opened to a thrilling variety of new flavours, tastes and textures.

The aim of *Feast* was to journey into the food history, cultures, life and religion of these amazing countries, all at street level, with real people—the locals who keep the traditions alive. Rather than visiting tourist haunts, we went off the beaten track, and were lucky enough to experience these countries in their true glory. When I think of my time in India, Morocco and Syria, I consider the amazing things I learned, the people I met, the food I tasted, and the new ingredients I discovered—as well as learning how to use familiar ingredients in new ways. By taking me deep into different cultures and lifestyles, my travels have highlighted for me what truly are the important things in life: family, food and good health.

The world is an amazing place. When you travel, experience everything you possibly can. Don't be afraid to try new foods—sheep's head and snails in Marrakech, for example, or brains in the Syrian Desert with the Bedouin tribes. I find when I try a new food, I later remember not just the way the food was cooked and where I was at the time, but the culture, tradition or ceremony that surrounded it.

In this book, I share with you some of the recipes that inspired me on my journey. I hope you enjoy them as much as I do.

For Wendy and Jack—for sharing the dream and all those beautiful memories

ARGANA
أركانة

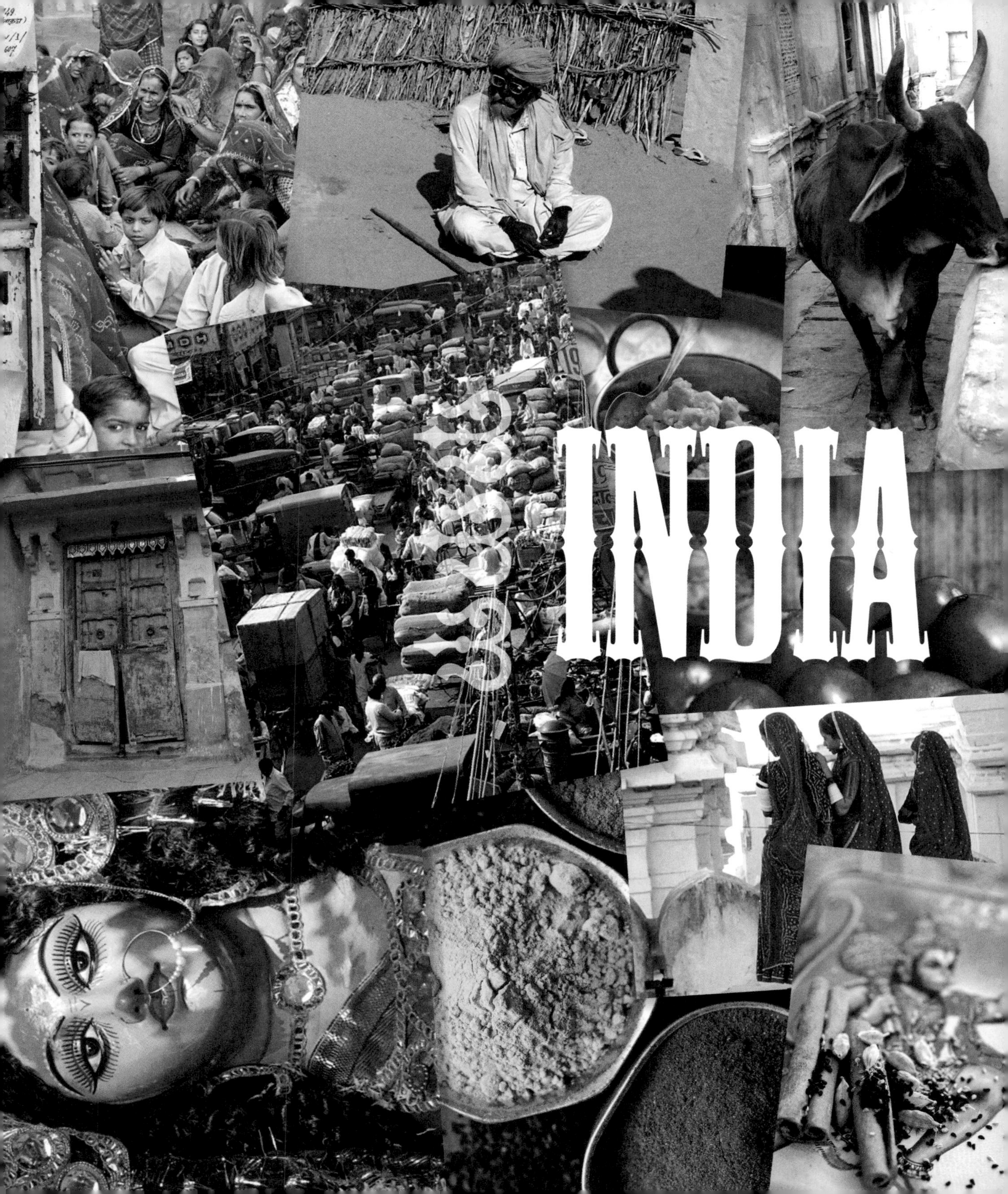
INDIA

India

India is vast, vibrant, diverse and exceptionally beautiful. When it was initially proposed that the first series of *Feast Bazaar* be filmed in India, I knew it was going to be a challenge. I spent a good deal of time reading up on India before I left. The more I read, the more it became apparent that this was going to be a journey that would affect me on many different levels.

After spending a day and a half travelling, we arrived in Kochi (Cochin), in the south, in the early hours of the morning. It was the end of the monsoon season and incredibly humid. All I could do was collapse into bed. I woke a few hours later to sunlight burning through the blinds. I went up on the roof of our guesthouse and looked out to see children playing cricket in the park against the backdrop of the Arabian Sea. This was my introduction to India.

That first morning I started with a ritualistic cup of fresh chai. Each morning that followed I would sit with the local fishermen and enjoy this sweet drink, sometimes flavoured with ginger or cardamom, which was a refreshing contrast to the intense heat. I have since made a chai ice cream, which is currently on my menu in the restaurant and has proved to be very popular (see recipe, page 51).

I was totally absorbed by the Indian way of life, yet it was also an emotional roller coaster. I was brought to tears on many occasions, but my travels also included lots of happy and memorable times. The friendships and the flavours of the food left me hungry for more.

India is now in my blood—from the lush green south, with its aromatic spice plantations, to the organized chaos of Mumbai, the enchanting desert villages of Rajasthan and the magical mayhem of Delhi. I plan to return and will continue to tell anyone who is planning to travel not to miss this amazing country.

Kerala—The Spice Bowl of India

The Indian state of Kerala is a thin strip of land wedged between the mountainous Western Ghats and the Arabian Sea. It's a wealthy state, with a rich and stormy past. For centuries it was a magnet for travellers and explorers alike. The Chinese, Portuguese, French, Dutch and English were all lured there in their search for spice, and each left their mark on Kerala's already colourful cuisine.

The port town of Kochi is the gateway to India's rich and lucrative spice trade; it's also renowned for its fresh seafood and coconut-infused cuisine. The harbour is lined with ancient fishing nets first erected by the Chinese during the reign of Kublai Khan, over 750 years ago. These nets reminded me of giant insects, ready to pounce on their prey. They are made from teak and bamboo and held together by rope made from the fibres of coconut husks. They're counterbalanced with large boulders, which hang precariously above the heads of the fishermen. I had a go at helping haul in the nets and retired after 15 minutes with blistered hands and a battered ego. All the Chinese fishing nets have a captain and crew, as with any boat, with the proceeds from the catch being shared among the hands.

The literal translation of 'Kerala' is 'Land of Coconuts'—in fact there's nowhere else in India that the humble coconut is so prized and put to so many uses. The flesh, milk and oil are the backbone of southern cooking.

The oil is used as a hair lotion, mixed with fragrant jasmine. The coconut shells are made into bowls for collecting rubber, among other uses. The husk is removed, placed in salt water for six months, then taken out, beaten and left to dry in the sun to produce fibres. The fibres are spun to produce rope, called coir, which is used to thatch boats and roofs, and also used to make rugs and carpets. Who would have thought the humble coconut had so many uses! New research has also found that coconut oil is a virtual powerhouse of compounds to help in the fight against autoimmune diseases, and scientists are looking into its role in the fight against HIV/AIDS.

Our next destination after Kochi was the lush green mountains of the Western Ghats that snake 1400 kilometres (870 miles) up the western coast of India, crossing three southern states including Kerala. The area is one of the world's most unique ecological havens, with an enormous variety of plants and wildlife. The Western Ghats ecosystems are genetic storehouses with untapped potential for biological and chemical development; it's also the most important watershed for peninsular India.

The main crops grown are tea, coffee, ginger, turmeric, cardamom and pepper—in fact, this region is called the Spice Bowl of India and happens to be one of the largest producers of spice in the world.

The amazing story of spices can be traced back to 6000 BC through references in the Vedic scriptures, the Bible and the Koran. In fact, the Egyptians had been using spices to embalm since 1200 BC and Middle Eastern traders had overland spice routes centuries before the Northern Europeans realized what they were missing out on. By the time spices had reached the European market, their price had inflated ten times over.

Christopher Columbus set off to find a sea route to the mysterious Malabar Coast of India and instead found the Americas. Eventually, Vasco da Gama was successful. When his crew landed they were heard to cry out, 'We've come in search of Christians and spices'. Over the following years, the Portuguese, Dutch and English fought among themselves for control of the spice trade. In the end, the English controlled the market through the East India Company.

Throughout this turbulent period, the most precious commodity of all was 'black gold'. These small berries were the most historically significant Indian spice of all—the king of spices, black pepper. Pepper brought bland food to life, it had preservative and medicinal powers, and was an ingredient in an antidote for poison. It was also used to pay rent and taxes; some slaves even bought their freedom with it. In fact, in 408 AD when the Barbarians conquered Rome, their ransom demand was 3000 pounds of black pepper. When the mummified body of one of the greatest Egyptian Pharaohs of all, Ramses the Second, was found, he had black pepper plugged inside his nose. Even in 1224 BC, black pepper was precious enough to take into the next world.

India's second royal spice is cardamom, a member of the ginger family. India traditionally exports cardamom to Middle Eastern countries, where it's used mainly in the preparation of *gahwa*, a strong cardamom/coffee concoction, which no Arab's day is complete without.

SERVES 4–6 AS A SNACK

1 kg (2 lb 4 oz) green (unripe) bananas
coconut oil or vegetable oil, for deep-frying
pinch of chilli powder

Salty and Spicy Banana Chips. We were in a little village in the spice mountains of the Western Ghats. We tasted some amazing street food, including food from a stall that was very popular with the locals. There was a guy with a huge wok of coconut oil, deep-frying banana chips. I bought a couple of packets and they were delicious, very salty and spicy.

Carefully peel the bananas, then thinly slice each one into rounds about ½ cm (¼ in) thick.

Fill a wok or deep heavy saucepan one-third full of oil and heat to 180°C (350°F), or until a cube of bread dropped inot the oil browns in 15 seconds.

Deep-fry the banana slices, in batches, making sure they have room to move and don't stick together. Fry for 3–5 minutes, or until a nice golden brown. Remove the chips with a slotted spoon and place on paper towel to drain off any excess oil.

Season well with sea salt and chilli powder and serve warm.

SERVES 4

2 tablespoons vegetable oil
½ teaspoon brown mustard seeds
½ teaspoon ground turmeric
1 teaspoon caster (superfine) sugar
2 long green chillies, finely chopped
550 g (1 lb 4 oz) floury potatoes, peeled, boiled and roughly chopped
1 handful coriander (cilantro) leaves, chopped

Batter
150 g (5½ oz) besan (chickpea flour)
¼ teaspoon ground cumin
¼ teaspoon baking powder
1 teaspoon olive oil
vegetable oil, for deep-frying

Bondas. These balls—which look a bit like doughnuts—are a popular snack in Kerala. The crew and I had these most mornings with a cup of chai. They are a great way to start the day, and fill you up until lunch. We would see the local fishermen sitting by the water eating these as the sun rose and a new day started.

Heat the oil in a frying pan and add the mustard seeds, turmeric, ¾ teaspoon salt, sugar and chilli. Cook for about 2–3 minutes to allow the flavours to open up and infuse. Add the potatoes, mashing as you mix, then stir through the coriander. Remove from the heat and allow the mixture to cool, then roll into 12 even-sized balls.

To make the batter, sift the besan, cumin and baking powder in a bowl and season. Add the olive oil and 125 ml (4 fl oz/½ cup) water and stir to form a thick batter.

Fill a wok or deep heavy-based saucepan one-third full of oil and heat to 180°C (350°C), or until a cube of bread dropped ino the oil browns in 15 seconds.

Dip the balls in the batter to coat. Deep-fry the bonda, in batches, for 3–5 minutes, or until golden brown and heated through. Remove with a slotted spoon and place on paper towel to drain off any excess oil. Serve immediately.

SERVES 4

300 g (10½ oz) radishes, trimmed and grated
6 medium roma (plum) tomatoes, seeded and finely chopped
1 long green chilli, finely chopped
1 red onion, finely chopped
1 telegraph (long) cucumber, peeled and finely chopped
1 baby cos (romaine) lettuce, thinly shredded
6 spring onions (scallions), thinly sliced
1 teaspoon finely grated fresh ginger
1 bunch flat-leaf (Italian) parsley, roughly chopped
finely grated zest of 1 lemon
2½ tablespoons lemon juice
125 ml (4 fl oz/½ cup) olive oil
sea salt and freshly ground black pepper, to taste

Tomato, Radish and Chilli Salad. I love fresh salad with any meal, and the simpler the better. This salad is great served with hot spicy food, and it's simply dressed with fresh lemon juice and olive oil.

Put all the ingredients in a bowl with 1 teaspoon salt and stir thoroughly to coat in the lemon juice and oil.

Season to taste and serve immediately. This dish tastes terrific with South Indian Fish Curry (see recipe, page 29).

SERVES 4

8 roma (plum) tomatoes, seeded and diced
1 red onion, finely diced
1 long red chilli, seeded and finely diced
1 telegraph (long) cucumber, peeled, seeded and diced
2 teaspoons cumin seeds, roasted and ground (see method, page 216)
1 teaspoon coriander seeds, roasted and ground (see method, page 216)
¼ teaspoon cayenne pepper
½ teaspoon freshly ground black pepper
3 tablespoons lime juice
1 large handful coriander (cilantro) leaves, finely chopped

Cachoombar. This salad is a great accompaniment to hot and spicy dishes.

Put all the ingredients in a bowl with 1 teaspoon salt and stir thoroughly to coat in the lime juice. Season to taste and serve immediately.

SERVES 4

250 g (9 oz) plain (all-purpose) flour
½ teaspoon caster (superfine) sugar
1 egg
4 tablespoons fresh goat's curd
2 tablespoons full-cream (whole) milk
1½ tablespoons butter, melted

Keralan Porotta. Next to rice, this bread was the most popular accompaniment. We liked it so much we ate it every day while travelling through Kerala. I remember sometimes buying it from a street hawker while filming, and eating it on its own with a cup of chai. The trick to getting this bread right is in the twist.

Mix the flour, sugar and 1 teaspoon salt together in a bowl. Make a well in the centre and add the egg, goat's curd, milk and ½ tablespoon melted butter, and stir to combine. Transfer to a floured bench and knead well for about 20 minutes, or until the dough is smooth and elastic.

Place the dough in a bowl, cover with a damp tea towel (dish towel) and set aside for 5 hours.

Knead again for about 10 minutes, then divide the dough into 8 balls about the size of a lemon. (These are so moreish that you may prefer to make 12 smaller balls so that you have extra to pass around to your guests.) Using a rolling pin, roll each one out to a form a disc shape, about 5 mm (¼ in) thick.

Brush each disc with melted butter on both sides and roll each one tightly into a thick rope. Keeping one end fixed, twist the rope in one direction, then shape the twisted rope into a coil, like a snake, starting from the inside and working outwards. Using the palm of your hand, gently flatten each one out against the bench until it is about 5 mm (¼ in) thick.

Preheat a barbecue hotplate or a non-stick frying pan to very hot. Working one at a time, brush both sides of the porotta generously with melted butter and cook for 2–3 minutes on each side, or until golden brown, being careful not to let them burn. Remove from the heat.

Stack the porotta on top of each other as you work, pushing them in from the sides with your hands to open up the layers and make them light. Serve immediately.

SERVES 4

Coriander Chutney
100 g (3½ oz) coriander (cilantro) leaves, roughly chopped
3 long green chillies, roughly chopped
1 garlic clove, roughly chopped
1 teaspoon lemon juice
1 teaspoon palm sugar (jaggery)

2 teaspoons finely grated fresh ginger
2 garlic cloves, finely chopped
4 dried red chillies, chopped
1 tablespoon malt vinegar
2 cloves
¼ teaspoon brown or black mustard seeds
½ teaspoon ground cumin
¼ teaspoon ground cinnamon
¼ teaspoon ground turmeric
2 tablespoons peanut oil
12 king prawns (shrimps), peeled and deveined, tails left intact
12 fresh curry leaves (see glossary)
1 small white onion, finely chopped
2 tomatoes, peeled and finely chopped (see method, page 215)
coriander (cilantro) sprigs, to garnish

Spiced Prawns. Prawns are a very popular seafood in Kerala, and the coriander chutney really completes this dish. It may look complex but, I assure you, once you have cooked it the first time you will want to do it again.

To make the coriander chutney, blend or grind all the ingredients with ½ teaspoon salt and 100 ml (3½ fl oz) water in a food processor or using a mortar and pestle, until a coarse paste forms. Set aside until needed. (Coriander chutney can be stored in an airtight container in the refrigerator for a couple of days.)

To make the spiced prawns, blend or grind the ginger, garlic, chilli, vinegar, cloves, mustard seeds, cumin, cinnamon, turmeric and ¼ teaspoon salt to a smooth paste in a food processor or using a mortar and pestle.

Heat the oil in a frying pan over medium–high heat and sauté the prawns for about 5 minutes, or until they turn pink and start to curl. Remove the prawns and set aside. Wipe the pan clean with a paper towel.

Heat a little more oil in the pan and add the curry leaves and onion. Cook for 5 minutes, or until golden brown. Add the tomatoes and cook for 2 minutes. Stir in the spice paste and cook for a further 3 minutes, or until the tomatoes start to soften. Return the prawns to the pan and gently cook for 2–3 minutes, until they are heated through. Remove from the heat.

Serve with Basmati Rice (see recipe, page 214), the coriander chutney and garnish with the coriander sprigs.

Like any good curry, the flavours are enhanced if left overnight. If you prefer to do this, allow the curry to cool slightly before covering and storing in the refrigerator. You will need to reheat the curry gently until the prawns are warmed through before serving.

SERVES 4

50 g (1¾ oz) freshly grated coconut or shredded coconut
1 red onion, finely chopped
1 long green chilli, thinly sliced
10 fresh curry leaves (see glossary)
¼ teaspoon black mustard seeds
500 g (1 lb 2 oz) Basmati Rice (see recipe, page 214)
1 handful fresh coriander (cilantro) leaves, finely chopped
3 tablespoons olive oil

Coconut Rice. This is one of the best rice dishes I think I've ever had. The flavour from the coconut, chilli and curry leaves is wonderful and complements the South Indian Fish Curry (see recipe, page 29) very well.

Heat a non-stick saucepan over medium heat and dry-fry the coconut for 3–5 minutes, or until lightly golden. Add the onion, chilli, curry leaves and mustard seeds and stir to combine. Reduce the heat and cook for 2 minutes, or until the coconut is golden brown. Remove from heat.

Add the coconut mixture, coriander and olive oil to the rice and stir thoroughly to combine. Season with sea salt, to taste. Serve immediately.

SERVES 4

Sauce
200 ml (7 fl oz) vegetable oil
½ teaspoon black mustard seeds
¼ teaspoon cumin seeds
¼ teaspoon ground turmeric
1 brown onion, finely chopped
2 garlic cloves, finely chopped
1 tablespoon finely grated ginger
2 long green chillies, thinly sliced on an angle
12 fresh curry leaves (see glossary)
400 ml (14 fl oz) coconut milk
500 ml (17 fl oz/2 cups) fish stock
4 roma (plum) tomatoes, peeled (see method, page 215) and diced

4 x 200 g (7 oz) boneless firm white fish fillets with the skin on, such as blue-eye trevalla or snapper
1 handful chopped coriander (cilantro) leaves

South Indian Fish Curry. This curry comes from the time I spent in Kerala while interviewing a Frenchman called Marc Delormé, who owned Casa Maria, a restaurant in Kochi. It has loads of flavour and a stunning creamy texture. When served with Coconut Rice (see recipe, page 26), the dish is complete. We serve this in the restaurant, and it has become very popular.

To make the sauce, heat 100 ml (3½ fl oz) of the oil in a large saucepan over medium heat. Add the mustard seeds, cumin seeds and turmeric and stir until they start to pop. Add the onion, garlic and ginger and cook gently for 5 minutes, or until the onion is translucent. Add the chilli and curry leaves and cook for a further 5 minutes. Add the coconut milk, fish stock, tomatoes and ¼ teaspoon salt and bring to the boil. Reduce the heat, then simmer for about 15 minutes, or until thickened. Remove from the heat and keep warm while preparing the fish. (This sauce can be prepared in advance and stored overnight, covered, in the refrigerator to enhance the flavours. You will have to gently reheat the sauce before serving.)

Heat the remaining oil in a frying pan over medium heat. Fry the fish, skin side down, for 3–5 minutes, or until golden brown. Turn over and cook the other side for about 2–3 minutes, or until cooked through. Add the coriander to the curry sauce, and pour over the fish. Serve with Coconut Rice (see recipe, page 26).

SERVES 6

6 long green chillies, thinly sliced
½ teaspoon ground turmeric
½ teaspoon ground coriander
2.5 cm (1 in) piece ginger, finely grated
5 garlic cloves
80 ml (2½ fl oz/⅓ cup) peanut oil
2 onions, finely chopped
1 cinnamon stick, broken
3 cloves
12 fresh curry leaves (see glossary)
6 chicken leg quarters (thighs and drumsticks), skinned
200 ml (7 fl oz) chicken stock
400 ml (14 fl oz) coconut cream
sea salt and freshly ground black pepper, to taste
chopped fresh chilli and coriander (cilantro) leaves, to garnish

Keralan-style Chicken Curry.

There are so many curries in so many styles. The great thing about curries in the south is that they generally include coconut cream, which helps balance out the spices for those who don't like it too hot.

Blend or grind the chilli, turmeric, coriander, ginger and garlic in a food processor or using a mortar and pestle. Add 1 teaspoon salt and 2 tablespoons of oil and continue mixing until a paste forms.

Heat the remaining oil in a large frying pan over medium heat. Add the onion, cinnamon and cloves and cook for about 5 minutes, or until softened. Add the curry leaves and spice paste and cook for 3 minutes, or until fragrant. Add the chicken and fry for 10–15 minutes, or until the chicken is golden brown.

Add the chicken stock, bring to a simmer and cook for a further 5 minutes, then add the coconut cream. Cover and gently simmer for about 15 minutes, or until the chicken is cooked. Remove from the heat.

Serve immediately, garnished with chilli and coriander. This dish tastes great with Coconut Rice (see recipe, page 26) and Keralan Porotta (see recipe, page 21).

SERVES 4

2 x 750 g (1 lb 10 oz) live crayfish
80 ml (2½ fl oz/⅓ cup) vegetable oil
1 tablespoon black mustard seeds
16 fresh curry leaves (see glossary)
2 red onions, finely chopped
250 g (9 oz) roma (plum) tomatoes, peeled (see method, page 215) and chopped
1 teaspoon ground turmeric
1 tablespoon red chilli powder
3 garlic cloves, finely chopped
5 cm (2 in) piece fresh ginger, finely grated
500 ml (17 fl oz/2 cups) coconut milk
Basmati Rice (see recipe, page 214), to serve

Indian-style Crayfish. Once I discovered this dish, I knew it would make its way onto my restaurant menu during summer—it tastes divine. Once you have all the preparation done, it is a very quick dish to cook.

Immobilize the crayfish by putting them in the freezer 1 hour before you plan to cook them.

To prepare the crayfish, hold the tail firmly in one hand with a tea towel (dish towel) and plunge a large, sharp kitchen knife into the midpoint, where the tail meets the head. Cut to separate, discarding the head. Cut each tail, in its shell, into six even pieces.

Heat the oil in a frying pan over medium heat. Add the mustard seeds and curry leaves and cook for about 2–3 minutes, or until the mustard seeds pop and become fragrant.

Add the onions and cook for 5 minutes, or until soft. Add the tomatoes, bring to the boil, then reduce the heat and simmer for 5–10 minutes, or until you have a sauce consistency. Stir in the turmeric and chilli powder and cook for 2 minutes, to allow the spices to open up. Add the garlic, ginger and coconut milk, bring to a simmer and cook for about 5 minutes, or until the sauce has thickened slightly. Add the crayfish to the pan and cook for about 10–15 minutes, or until the meat is opaque.

Serve immediately on individual plates with Basmati Rice on the side.

SERVES 8

Cardamom Panna Cotta
625 ml (21½ fl oz/2½ cups) full-cream (whole) milk
170 ml (5½ fl oz/⅔ cup) pouring (whipping) cream
125 g (4½ oz) caster (superfine) sugar
10 green cardamom pods, bruised
1 vanilla bean, split, seeds scraped
6 (2 g) gelatine leaves (see glossary)
20 pistachio nuts, roughly chopped, to garnish

Poached Pears and Syrup
500 g (1 lb 2 oz/2¼ cups) caster (superfine) sugar
8 green cardamom pods, bruised
2 oranges, cut into quarters
4 star anise
1 vanilla bean, split
4 beurre bosc or corella pears, peeled and cored

Cardamom Panna Cotta with Poached Pears. Panna cotta is a great dessert—simple, light and easy to make. Brent Love, my pastry chef, devised this dish. The delicate flavour of the cardamom takes me back to the spice mountains in the Western Ghats. We stayed at the cardamom research centre and saw the work that goes into providing us with such a remarkable spice. The Indian people have such a passion for spices. When I asked where India would be without spices, I was told there would be no India, and I can truly believe that.

To make the panna cotta, put a saucepan over medium heat and add the milk, cream, sugar, cardamom and vanilla bean and seeds. Bring to the boil, then reduce the heat and simmer for 10 minutes.

Soak the gelatine in cold water for 5 minutes until completely soft, then squeeze the excess water out of the leaves. Add them to the pan with the milk mixture and whisk until combined. Remove from the heat and pass through a fine sieve into a clean jug. Pour into eight individual ½-cup dariole moulds and refrigerate overnight to set—it should still be slightly wobbly.

To make the poached pear syrup, put the sugar, cardamom, oranges, star anise, vanilla bean and 1.5 litres (52 fl oz/6 cups) water in a saucepan over high heat and bring to the boil. Reduce the heat, add the pears and simmer for 10 minutes, or until tender. Remove the pears from the syrup and refrigerate until needed.

Continue cooking the syrup over medium heat for about 15 minutes, or until the liquid reduces to a syrup. Remove from the heat and allow to cool.

To remove the panna cotta from the mould, run a knife around the rim, or dip the mould into hot water for 5 seconds and invert onto a serving dish. Gently lift off the mould.

Cut the cooked pears into thin wedges and scatter around each panna cotta. Spoon the pear syrup over the top and garnish with pistachio nuts.

SERVES 2

300 ml (10½ fl oz) fresh pineapple juice
1 cinnamon stick
2 green cardamom pods
2 cloves
6 mint leaves
1½ tablespoons lime juice
2 vodka shots (optional)
ice, to serve

Spiced Pineapple Juice. There is nothing better on a hot day than fresh juice on ice and, as always in India, spices are added. This drink also tastes great with an alcoholic twist.

Heat half of the pineapple juice in a saucepan over low–medium heat. Add the cinnamon, cardamom and cloves and simmer for about 10 minutes to allow the flavours to infuse. Remove from the heat and cool.

Pour the mixture into a large jug and add the remaining pineapple juice, along with the mint leaves and lime juice. Add the vodka, if using, and stir to combine. Top up the jug with ice. Stir well and serve.

SERVES 2

Spice Mix
1¼ cinnamon sticks
6 cloves
4 black peppercorns
6 green cardamom pods
1 teaspoon fennel seeds
1 teaspoon ground ginger

500 ml (17 fl oz/2 cups) full-cream (whole) milk
2 tablesoons caster (superfine) sugar
2 black-tea bags

Masala Chai—Spiced Tea. Each morning in India I would navigate my way through the streets to the nearest chai cart and found I never had to go far; being a staple drink, these carts were everywhere. One time, while filming in the Western Ghats, we were invited into a family home and offered chai. The hostess went outside, milked the cow in the garden and made us chai with fresh milk—it was heavenly.

To make the spice mix, dry-roast all the ingredients except the ginger in a small frying pan for about 2–3 minutes over gentle heat, or until the spices become aromatic. Remove from the heat, stir in the ginger and allow to cool.

Grind the spice mix into a powder using a mortar and pestle or a spice grinder. (Any leftover spice can be stored in an airtight container for up to 3 months. This amount of spice mix will make approximately 18–20 mugs of chai.)

To make the chai, put the milk in a saucepan and place over medium heat. Add the sugar, stirring to dissolve, and bring the milk to the boil. Once at boiling point, remove the saucepan from the heat, add the tea bags and allow to infuse for a few minutes—you need to make a reasonably strong brew. Remove the tea bags and discard.

Stir ¼ teaspoon of the spice mix into the saucepan and return to the heat. Bring back up to the boil. You can either pour it into two mugs as is, or use a stick blender and mix to create a froth on top before serving.

A ROYAL SPICE

While pepper is considered the king of spices in the Spice Mountains of the Western Ghats, cardamom is known as the queen. A member of the ginger family, cardamom pods have to be hand-picked before they ripen and split. The intensive labour required in this process makes it the second most costly spice in the world, after saffron. Once picked, cardamom pods are dried for 36 hours in a curing chamber. The whole pods are used in pilafs and curries, and the ground seeds in sauces, spice blends, desserts and beverages. As well as adding flavour, cardamom reputedly stimulates the appetite, refreshes the mind and even relieves gas!

Mumbai—Diwali in the City of Dreams

You don't visit Mumbai: it visits you. Mumbai, once known as Bombay, is now home to 17 million people—a city with a passion for life, which is chaotic, colourful, confronting and always intriguing. The longer you stay there, the better Mumbai gets.

It is predicted that over 30 million people will live in Mumbai by 2020. This commercial capital of India is rapidly becoming one of the largest populated cities in the world. About 7 million people commute to work from the suburbs into the city every day. It is also home to Bollywood, one of the most thriving film industries in the world, with about a thousand movies made each year.

This 'City of Dreams' lures some of the richest and poorest of India to a vibrant metropolis that is literally bursting at the seams. Kiosks, tea carts and mobile snack vendors line the streets and pavements. Smoke billows from giant woks and hotplates; pastries and deep-fried vegetables swim in seas of spice-infused coconut oil.

Mumbai is a city on the run, with no time to stop and stare—unless food is involved. Socializing is an important part of Indian culture; they love to mix and chat. And there's no better place to do this than on the streets and beaches. Food is very important, both religiously and culturally. At home people eat very simply, but when they go out it's both lavish and wholesome.

In just about every aspect of Indian life you'll find a religious influence, and food—in the way it's eaten, presented and shared with others—is a natural way of expressing one's faith. Food is also an opportunity for people to make an offering to their Gods. It is believed that by God's mercy and generosity the monsoon comes and the rains refresh and fertilize the fields and farms of India. Whatever is grown is a gift from the Almighty and the first grains are always given back to God in the form of offerings at local temples.

The most important holy festival in India is Diwali, known as 'The Festival of Lights' or the Indian New Year festival. It involves five days of revelry and rituals celebrated during October/November, with festivities even spilling over into adjoining countries.

Although Diwali is essentially a Hindu celebration, people of every religion can't help but get involved in India's most joyous festival. A family in Mumbai will celebrate the festival in a very different way to a family in Kerala or a small village in Rajasthan. Like most events in India, the festival hinges on the lunar cycle. On the dark, moonless night of Diwali literally millions of tonnes of firecrackers are set off throughout the country. Some are chosen for their colourful displays, which bring light to the world, while others are used purely for their loud explosions, symbolizing the triumph of good over evil.

During Diwali it is believed Lakshmi, the Goddess of Wealth, only visits homes and shops that are well lit to impart her much-desired blessings of financial abundance. Homes and businesses are festooned with lamps, as well as flowers and paper chains, and doors are left wide open all night to welcome her.

You don't have to prepare a great feast: it's said that even the simplest food will please the Gods. The offering of sweets plays an important role in Indian culture, especially during Diwali. My host in Mumbai, Vimla Patil, is a well-known media spokesperson, author and women's rights campaigner who has also written more than fifteen cookbooks. She told me that sweets are supposed to make your life sweet, and when you give someone sweets it means 'I wish for you that your life will be sweet'. In India, they are also considered a luxurious present because they are more expensive than savoury foods, and when making them most people will use the best ingredients (saffron, almonds and pistachios) they can afford.

During Diwali, businesses present employees with gifts and bonuses, donations are made to temples and lavish meals are cooked for the less fortunate. Like the sweets on offer, I found Diwali highly addictive and the atmosphere of generosity very humbling to be a part of.

The essence of Diwali isn't all about grand gestures—it can be expressed very simply by lighting a lamp at home. It's really about the desire to make life better for everyone, and is summed up in a Diwali prayer: 'In the human race let there be light where there is darkness, let there be truth where there is untruth and let there be nectar instead of death.'

SERVES 4

Dosas
300 g (10½ oz/1½ cups) basmati rice
125 g (4½ oz/½ cup) split urad dal (see glossary)
1 long green chilli, finely diced
1 red onion, finely diced
100 ml (3½ fl oz) vegetable oil

Masala Filling
2 teaspoons split urad dal (see glossary)
1 kg (2 lb 4 oz) all-purpose potatoes, peeled and diced into 1.5 cm (5/8 in) cubes
4 tablespoons vegetable oil
2 teaspoons cumin seeds
1 teaspoon brown mustard seeds
15 fresh curry leaves (see glossary)
5 dried long red chillies
1 teaspoon ground turmeric
1 brown onion, finely chopped
2 teaspoons finely grated fresh ginger
3 roma (plum) tomatoes, diced
1 handful coriander (cilantro) leaves, roughly chopped

Dosas with Masala Filling. Dosas are like very crisp, thin pancakes often served with a potato masala filling and eaten for breakfast. I devoured many of them travelling through India and one was never enough. They do take a while to prepare but, once made, they taste delicious. The dosas will need to be prepared the day before you wish to eat them.

To make the dosas, put the rice and dal in a bowl and cover with water. Soak for 6 hours. Drain, then place in a food processor and blend to form a fine paste. Add 1 teaspoon salt and add just enough water to create a smooth pancake-style batter. Transfer to a bowl, cover with plastic wrap and refrigerate overnight.

The next day, add the chilli and onion to the batter and stir to combine.

Heat the oil in a non-stick frying pan over medium heat and drop 3 tablespoons of batter at a time into the base of the pan, gently tilting the pan to create a thin crepe. Cook for 1 minute on each side, or until a light golden brown. As you finish each dosa, transfer to a plate in a low oven to keep warm while preparing the filling. You should make 8 dosas in total.

To make the masala filling, soak the dal in hot water for about 15 minutes, then drain.

Put the potatoes into a saucepan of boiling salted water and cook for 10 minutes, or until tender. Remove from heat, drain and set aside.

Heat the oil in a frying pan over medium heat, then add the cumin and mustard seeds. Once they start to pop, add the curry leaves, dal, chillies, turmeric and onion. Cook, stirring often, for about 10 minutes, or until the onion is soft. Add the ginger, tomato, potato and 1 teaspoon salt. Mix well and cook for a further 10 minutes, or until the potato is tender. Mix in the coriander just before you are ready to serve.

Place two dosas on each plate, add a couple of tablespoons of the masala filling and roll up, to serve. Dosas taste great with a cup of Masala Chai (see recipe, page 37).

SERVES 4

4 corn cobs
100 g (3½ oz) butter, softened
hot chilli powder, to taste
2 limes, cut into wedges, to serve

Grilled Corn on the Cob with Lime and Chilli. While interviewing on Chawpati Beach one evening, we stopped at a rickety old hawker stand on the beach. The aroma of corn roasted on open coals was mouthwatering. The corn was basted with butter and then finished with fresh lime juice, hot chilli and salt.

Heat a barbecue chargrill plate to medium-high. Remove any husk or fibres from the corn.

Put the corn on the grill plate and cook for 8–10 minutes, brushing with the softened butter and turning regularly until the corn is tender and golden brown all over. Remove and season with the chilli powder and salt, to taste. Serve with the lime wedges for squeezing over.

SERVES 4

5 long red chillies, seeded and finely chopped
1 teaspoon coriander seeds
5 black peppercorns
1 teaspoon ground turmeric
1 brown onion, finely chopped
1 tablespoon grated fresh ginger
4 garlic cloves, finley chopped
1 teaspoon tamarind concentrate (see glossary)
1 teaspoon soft brown sugar
2 tablespoons vegetable oil, plus extra, for frying
4 x 200 g (7 oz) firm white fish fillets, such as jewfish, blue-eye trevalla or sea bass

Crisp Spiced Fish. I first had this dish at Mahesh Restaurant in Mumbai. There it is fried in coconut oil, which does change the flavour slightly, but for this recipe I have used vegetable oil.

Put all the spices, onion, ginger, garlic, tamarind, sugar, vegetable oil and ¼ teaspoon salt into a food processor or mortar and pestle and blend or grind to make a paste.

Coat both sides of the fish fillets in the paste and leave to marinate in a non-metallic dish for at least 2 hours, covered in the refrigerator.

Heat the extra oil in a frying pan over medium heat and cook the fish for 3–4 minutes on each side, or until the fish flakes easily with a fork and is just opaque. (The spices will darken in colour as the fish cooks.)

Serve immediately with Cachoombar salad (see recipe, page 20).

SERVES 4

2 x 200 g (7 oz) skinless free-range chicken breasts, cut into 2½ cm (1 in) dice
2 tablespoons plain yoghurt
3 garlic cloves, very finely chopped
2 teaspoons finely grated ginger
¼ teaspoon garam masala (see recipe, page 60)
200 g (7 oz) butter
90 g (3¼ oz/⅓ cup) tomato paste (concentrated purée)
200 ml (7 fl oz) thick (double/heavy) cream
2 teaspoons fenugreek seeds, roasted (see method, page 216) and crushed (see glossary)
3 long green chillies, thinly sliced lengthways

Butter Chicken. I love this dish, with its mild flavour. You need to start this dish the day before you want to serve it. Don't forget to have on hand plenty of bread to mop up the sauce.

Combine the chicken, yoghurt, half the garlic, 1 teaspoon ginger and garam masala in a non-metallic bowl and mix well. Cover and marinate for at least 6 hours, or overnight in the refrigerator.

Preheat the grill (broiler) to medium. Place the chicken in a shallow roasting tray in a single layer and grill (broil) for 15 minutes, turning halfway through cooking, or until golden brown.

Meanwhile, gently melt the butter in a frying pan over low–medium heat and add the remaining garlic and ginger. Mix well, stir in the tomato paste and cook gently for about 3 minutes, or until fragrant. Add the cream, mix well and simmer for a further 2–3 minutes. Add the fenugreek and ¾ teaspoon salt and mix well.

Add the cooked chicken and chilli to the sauce and gently mix to coat the chicken. Simmer for 2–3 minutes to allow the flavours to infuse and the chicken to heat through.

Serve immediately with Basmati Rice (see recipe, page 214).

SERVES 6

½ cinnamon stick
3 cloves
2 black peppercorns
3 green cardamom pods
½ teaspoon fennel seeds
½ teaspoon ground ginger
455 ml (16 fl oz) full-cream (whole) milk
300 ml (10½ fl oz) pouring (whipping) cream
9 egg yolks
200 g (7 oz) caster (superfine) sugar
250 ml (9 fl oz/1 cup) hot and strong black-tea, such as English Breakfast

Tea Syrup
800 ml (28 fl oz) black-tea, such as English Breakfast
150 g (5½ oz) caster (superfine) sugar

Masala Chai Ice Cream. In India, every cup of chai contains a lot of sugar. When I made this ice cream, I needed to re-create that sweetness but didn't want it to be so sweet that the flavours were lost. As a result I made a tea syrup to complete the dish and allow the spices to shine through.

Put the cinnamon, cloves, peppercorns, cardamom and fennel seeds into a frying pan and dry-fry for 2–3 minutes, or until they are aromatic. Remove from the heat, then mix in the ginger. Allow to cool, then grind to a fine powder using a mortar and pestle or spice grinder.

Put the milk and cream in a saucepan over medium heat and bring to the boil. In a separate bowl, whisk the egg yolks and sugar together until pale in colour. Add the yolks and sugar to the milk and cream, whisking continuously over medium heat. Keep whisking the mixture until it starts to thicken (this can take up to 10 minutes), then immediately remove from the heat and transfer to a large mixing bowl. Add the tea and the spice mix, stirring to combine. Allow to cool, then cover and refrigerate for 24 hours for the flavours to develop.

Transfer to an ice-cream machine and freeze according to the manufacturer's instructions. Alternatively, transfer to a shallow metal tray and freeze, whisking every couple of hours until frozen and creamy. Freeze until ready to serve.

To make the tea syrup, place the tea and sugar in a saucepan over high heat and stir to dissolve the sugar. Bring to the boil and cook for about 15 minutes, or until the liquid is a syrupy consistency. Remove from the heat and allow to cool. The syrup can be made in advance and stored in an airtight container in the refrigerator for 2–3 days.

To serve, scoop the ice cream into a bowl and pour some chilled tea syrup over the top.

SERVES 2–4

2½ cm (1 in) fresh ginger, grated
50 g (1¾ oz/¼ cup) caster (superfine) sugar
125 ml (4 fl oz/½ cup) lemon juice
1½ tablespoons lime juice
1 green cardamom pod
3 black peppercorns
pinch of cumin seeds
1 lemon, sliced, to serve
1 lime, sliced, to serve
fresh mint sprigs, to serve

Lemon, Lime and Ginger Soda. This is an Indian version of lemonade. On a hot day in summer, it's very refreshing, and with the spices and ginger added it's quite unique.

Place the ginger, sugar, citrus juices, cardamom, peppercorns, cumin seeds and 500 ml (17 fl oz/ 2 cups) water in a large saucepan over medium heat. Stir until the sugar has dissolved. Bring to the boil, then reduce the heat and simmer on a very low heat for 30 minutes to allow the flavours to infuse. Cool slightly, then strain and refrigerate until well chilled.

Place some ice in a jug with the lemon and lime slices and mint. Top with the lemon-lime mixture and stir to combine. Pour into glasses filled with ice.

SERVES 4

100 g (3½ oz) dark chocolate (70% cocoa)
100 ml (3½ fl oz) pouring (whipping) cream
100 ml (3½ fl oz) full-cream (whole) milk
100 g (3½ oz) sweetened cocoa powder
½ teaspoon ground cinnamon
60 g (2¼ oz/¼ cup) demerara sugar (see glossary)
1 dried red chilli
chilli flakes, to garnish
grated chocolate, to garnish

Hot or Cold Chilli Chocolate. This drink from Mumbai is really a spicy milkshake that can be served hot or cold. It is quite refreshing, with a bit of a kick.

Break the chocolate into small pieces and place in a saucepan with the remaining ingredients except the chilli flakes and grated chocolate.

Place over low–medium heat and stir constantly until the chocolate has almost melted. Simmer gently for about 3 minutes, whisking until all the chocolate has dissolved and the mix is a smooth, even colour.

If you are serving hot, strain the mixture immediately through a fine sieve and pour into espresso cups. If you are serving cold, remove from the heat, strain and allow to cool, then refrigerate for 2 hours, or until chilled. Garnish with a sprinkle of chilli flakes and grated chocolate on top.

SERVES 6 AS A SNACK

1 teaspoon unsalted butter
200 g (7 oz) muscovado sugar (see glossary)
200 g (7 oz/1 ¼ cups) unsalted peanuts, crushed

Caramelized Peanuts. Street hawkers were selling these in India, and the nuts reminded me of something similar I ate as a child. Many Indians have a sweet tooth (as did the film crew!) so this snack was very popular.

Place the butter, sugar and 2 tablespoons water into a large heavy-based saucepan over medium heat, stirring just until the sugar dissolves. Bring to the boil and cook for 10 minutes, or until a toffee syrup forms. Add the peanuts and mix to combine. Remove from the heat and pour the mixture onto a sheet of baking paper. Allow to cool.

Serve broken into bite-sized pieces. Caramelized nuts can be stored in an airtight container for 2–3 weeks. (You can substitute peanuts in this recipe with almonds or cashews if you prefer.)

Old Delhi

At first I found Delhi confronting; I was overwhelmed by the crowds but, after walking around for a day or two, I was totally hooked—Delhi is a crazy, magnificent and chaotic city.

To truly appreciate Delhi, you have to know a bit about its colourful past. India's capital has had many reincarnations; it has been invaded, conquered, ransacked, torn down and rebuilt by a succession of rulers and dynasties. But, luckily, many beautiful mosques, tombs, monuments and forts have survived those turbulent times.

It seems that everybody has had a shot at Delhi—the Parthians, Scythians, Turks, Afghans, Moguls and Britons—but out of all the conquerors, the Moguls left the most lasting impressions. Old Delhi was the Muslim capital of India for more than 200 years before the British Raj.

In Old Delhi you'll find one of the world's largest spice markets. It is an aromatic wonderland, a winding labyrinth of congested alleyways, old warehouses and overflowing bazaars that has been operating for centuries. Merchants from Northern Asia, China, Persia and the Middle East traded spices, dried fruits and nuts, adding to India's already exotic flavours. Today, spice trading is still big business; over sixty spice varieties are grown there, supplying over half the world's demand, and consuming 3 060 000 tonnes (3 million tons) itself each year.

It is impossible to talk about spices without talking about how they are used to flavour so many different Indian dishes. When most Westerners think of Indian food, they think 'curry'. However, interestingly, the word curry doesn't rate a mention in any of India's culinary dictionaries nor, for that matter, does curry powder exist in Indian kitchens. Actually, curry is taken from the Tamil word 'kari', which means sauce. When you cook with various spices, it's not simply a matter of throwing a few randomly into a pot. As many traditional Indian meals will testify, there is an incredible amount of skill in the way that individual spices are roasted, ground and blended to create subtle aromas, textures and flavours.

In Delhi, I tried one of India's oldest and favourite addictions: the chewing of paan. The astringent leaf of the betel tree is smothered in lime paste, topped with betel nut and a mixture of sweet and aromatic spices, and then conserves are added. These could include fennel, cardamom seeds, coconut shreds, candied rosebuds or scented anise. There are literally hundreds of paan ingredient possibilities, although I have to say it's definitely an acquired taste.

I also drank copious quantities of chai, and no two cups were ever the same. Although it's usually very strong, milky and extremely sweet, depending on where you are in India, different spices are added. I tasted versions which included various combinations of cardamom, ginger and masala chai to a most refreshing black pepper chai.

When India gained independence from the British in 1947, the new country of Pakistan was created. This new border divided the Punjab, forcing many Punjabi Sikhs to resettle in other parts of India, particularly Delhi. This changed the dynamic of the city and also added to the already diverse culinary fabric of its streets.

While in Delhi, I visited my first Sikh temple. The Sikhs, or 'seekers of light', believe in the one formless God and follow the teachings of a succession of ten gurus, each representing divine qualities such as humility, equality, justice and mercy. The largest Sikh temple in Delhi is the Gurudwara Bangla Sahib. Before entering the temple, shoes are removed, feet are washed and heads covered as a sign of respect.

Gurudwaras, or temples, are open to all communities and castes; all people are considered equal, irrespective of their standing in the world outside. One of the important principals of the Sikh religion is the sharing of food. The Sikhs fulfil this divine duty through the preparation of free meals, which are traditionally vegetarian. Staffed solely by volunteers, the Gurudwara Bangla Sahib serves a staggering 70 000 meals every day. These community dining halls, or *langars*, are open around the clock, every day of the year. Huge brass pots are stirred constantly with giant paddles. They contain dal and vegetable curries that are served with fresh bread. They are funded by donations, as well as contributions of flour, lentils and spices, and it's considered an honour and spiritually rewarding for devotees to work in the kitchen and dining hall. Although it's buzzing with activity, the atmosphere is serenely peaceful. As I sat and ate with my fellow diners, I felt deeply touched by the generosity and kindness of the Sikh community, and the food was as memorable as it was simple.

MAKES 6 TABLESPOONS

3 teaspoons cloves
6 bay leaves
6 green cardamom pods, seeds only
18 black cardamom pods, seeds only
3 teaspoons caraway seeds
36 black peppercorns
1½ teaspoons freshly grated nutmeg

Garam Masala. An integral ingredient in most curry dishes in the north, 'garam masala' means 'hot spices' and, as the name suggests, it brings heat to a dish.

You can buy garam masala mixes today, but they can vary in taste. The best way to understand how spices work, and how good the flavours can be, is to prepare your own. Once you try it, you won't go back.

Heat a frying pan over medium heat and add all the spices except the nutmeg. Dry-fry for about 5 minutes to release all the flavours.

Remove from the heat and add the nutmeg. Grind to a fine powder using a mortar and pestle or a spice grinder.

Garam masala can be stored in an airtight container for up to 3 months. Spices will lose their flavour over time, so it is best to grind the them in small amounts to maximize their flavours.

SERVES 4

3 tablespoons vegetable oil
1 large brown onion, finely chopped
3 long green chillies, finely chopped
3 garlic cloves, finely chopped
400 g (14 oz) potatoes, peeled and cut into 2 cm (¾ in) dice
300 g (10½ oz) cauliflower, cut into small florets
1½ teaspoons ground turmeric
½ teaspoon ground cumin
½ teaspoon ground coriander
½ teaspoon garam masala (see recipe, page 60)
2 tablespoons butter
1 teaspoon finely grated ginger

Aloo Gobhi—Spiced Cauliflower and Potato. Maybe it's the British in me, but I love cauliflower and am always looking for new ways to cook and eat it. Aloo gobhi is perfect served on its own and is great for vegetarians. The textures and flavour combine well and like all good recipes this can be tasted in every mouthful.

Heat the oil in a frying pan over medium heat and add the onion, chilli, garlic and potato. Cook for 5 minutes, or until the onion is translucent.

Add the cauliflower and fry until lightly golden. Add the turmeric, cumin, coriander, garam masala and ¾ teaspoon salt. Cook for a further 5 minutes, stirring gently, or until aromatic.

Add the butter, ginger and 80 ml (2½ fl oz/ ⅓ cup) water and bring to the boil. Reduce the heat and continue to simmer for 5–8 minutes, or until the potato is tender. Remove from the heat, season to taste and serve.

SERVES 6 AS A SNACK

4 medium all-purpose potatoes, peeled
250 g (9 oz/2 cups) plain (all-purpose) flour
½ teaspoon ajowan seeds (see glossary)
125 ml (4 fl oz/½ cup) vegetable oil, plus extra, for deep-frying
½ teaspoon cumin seeds
½ teaspoon coriander seeds
1 teaspoon ground ginger
1 teaspoon turmeric
¼ teaspoon chilli powder
50 g (1¾ oz/⅓ cup) green peas

Samosas. These are great to serve as a snack—not only do they taste great but they are surprisingly simple to prepare. After spending time in the spice markets in Delhi I came to really appreciate these wonderfully spiced samosas.

Cook the potatoes whole in boiling salted water for 12–15 minutes, or until tender. Drain well, then cut into 1 cm (½ in) dice and set aside.

Combine the flour, ajowan seeds and ½ teaspoon salt in a bowl. Add 1 tablespoon of the oil and mix until a firm dough forms.

Divide the dough into 12 even-sized balls. Slightly flatten each ball on a lightly floured surface and roll into rounds with a 10 cm (4 in) diameter, and 5 mm (¼ in) thick. Cut each round in half, sprinkle with a little flour and set aside.

To make the filling, heat the remaining oil in a large non-stick frying pan over medium heat. Add the cumin and coriander seeds, ginger, turmeric, chilli powder and ¼ teaspoon salt. Stirring constantly, cook for 1–2 minutes or until aromatic. Add the potatoes and peas and stir to thoroughly combine. Cook for 2–3 minutes, or until heated through. Set aside and allow to cool.

To prepare the samosas, line the longer edge of each pastry round along your fingers, resting in your palm. Apply a little water along the edges and form the pastry into a cone shape by pulling one shorter side over the other and sealing the outside edge. Fill with potato mixture through the opening at the top, then press the top edges together forming a fat triangular pocket.

Fill a wok or large heavy-based saucepan one-third full of oil and heat to 180°C (350°F), or until a cube of bread dropped into the oil browns in 15 seconds. Deep-fry the samosas, in batches, for 5 minutes each, or until they are golden brown. Remove and drain on paper towel.

Serve the samosas with Indian Tomato Chutney (see recipe, page 81), for dipping.

MAKES 6

150 g (5½ oz/1 cup) wholemeal (whole-wheat) flour, plus extra for dusting
¼ teaspoon ground turmeric
30 g (1 oz) fenugreek leaves, finely chopped, or 2 tablespoons of ground dried fenugreek (see glossary)
½ teaspoon mild chilli powder
½ teaspoon ground coriander
½ teaspoon cumin seeds
1 teaspoon finely grated fresh ginger
3 tablespoons peanut oil

Thelpas—Unleavened Fenugreek Flatbread. The breads I tried throughout India were amazing, and great for mopping up all the sauces, pickles and dals. *Thelpas* are baked flatbreads, similar to chapatis. This recipe, which I like very much, uses fenugreek leaves. If you can't find those, you can use dried fenugreek instead.

Mix the flour, turmeric, fenugreek leaves, chilli powder, coriander, cumin seeds and ginger together with 1 tablespoon of the oil in a bowl. Add 100 ml (3½ fl oz) water and mix until it just comes together. Knead for about 5 minutes on a lightly floured surface until it forms a soft dough.

Place in a bowl and leave for 5 minutes, covered with a damp tea towel (dish towel).

Divide the dough into 6 even-sized balls. Take one ball at a time and dust it with the extra flour. Keep the others covered with the damp cloth so they don't dry out. Roll each ball into a 12 cm (4½ in) disc about 2 mm (1/16 in) thick.

Heat a barbecue hotplate or large heavy-based frying pan over medium–high heat. When hot, add a little of the remaining oil and cook the flatbreads, one or two at a time, for about 1–2 minutes on each side, or until golden. Keep pressing the bread down with a spatula to keep them flat and ensure they cook through. Place on a tray and cover with foil while you cook the rest.

You can serve thelpas on their own or to accompany a good curry.

SERVES 4 AS A SNACK

1 bunch English spinach, washed, drained and coarsely chopped
½ teaspoon ajowan seeds (see glossary)
2 pinches bicarbonate of soda (baking soda)
200 g (7 oz) besan (chickpea flour)
vegetable oil, for deep-frying
sea salt and freshly ground black pepper, to taste

Spinach Pakoras. India has so much to offer when it comes to street food and it is available from sunrise to sunset. Spinach pakoras are the perfect size for snacking on and are a popular temptation on the streets of Delhi.

Mix together the spinach, ajowan seeds, bicarbonate of soda, besan and a pinch of salt. Leave the mixture to sit for 5 minutes.

Using lightly floured hands, mould the mixture into 8 even-sized balls.

Heat the oil in a wok or large heavy-based saucepan to 180°C (350°F), or until a cube of bread dropped into the oil browns in 15 seconds. Deep-fry the pakoras, in batches, for 2–3 minutes each, or until golden and cooked. Drain on paper towel, season to taste and serve immediately.

MAKES APPROXIMATELY 4 X 250 ML (9 FL OZ) JARS

1 cauliflower, cut into small florets
1 telegraph (long) cucumber, peeled, seeded and cut into 1 cm (½ in) dice
3 large brown onions, cut into 1 cm (½ in) dice
8 large French shallots, cut into 1 cm (½ in) dice
500 ml (17 fl oz/2 cups) white wine vinegar
300 ml (10½ fl oz) malt vinegar
¼ teaspoon chopped dried red chilli
350 g (12 oz/1½ cups) caster (superfine) sugar
50 g (1¾ oz) brown mustard seeds
1 tablespoon ground turmeric
3 tablespoons cornflour (cornstarch)
sea salt and freshly ground black pepper, to taste

Mustard Pickle. In the markets of Delhi, you'll find whole stalls devoted to pickles. I love pickles, as they complement many foods, such as fish, curries and dals, very well. You need to start this recipe a day before you wish to serve it, as the cauliflower is salted and left for 24 hours.

Put the cauliflower into a colander, sprinkle with 1 teaspoon salt and leave to drain for 24 hours. Rinse well under cold running water and pat dry.

Put the cucumber in a colander, sprinkle with 1 teaspoon salt and leave for 10–15 minutes. Rinse with cold running water and pat dry.

Mix the cauliflower, cucumber, onions and shallots in a large non-metallic bowl.

Put the white wine vinegar, malt vinegar and chilli in a saucepan over high heat and bring to the boil. Remove from the heat and allow to stand for 30 minutes.

Mix together the sugar, mustard seeds, turmeric and cornflour in a separate bowl. Stir in just enough of the vinegar mixture, a little at a time, to form a smooth paste.

Return the remaining vinegar mixture in the pan to the heat and bring to the boil. Pour in the paste and stir to combine. Reduce the heat and simmer gently for 3 minutes, or until the mixture has thickened.

Pour the vinegar mixture over the vegetables in the bowl and mix well. Transfer the pickles into sterilized airtight jars (see method, page 216) while the mixture is still hot. Seal immediately and allow to cool to room temperature.

Mustard pickles will keep for 2 months after opening stored in the refrigerator.

MAKES 2 X 250 ML (9 FL OZ) JARS

900 g (2 lb) green (unripe) mangoes, peeled
125 ml (4 fl oz/½ cup) peanut oil
1½ teaspoons brown mustard seeds
¾ teaspoon ground turmeric
3 teaspoons hot chilli powder
1½ tablespoons soft brown sugar

Mango Pickle. No Indian meal is complete without a pickle, and one we all know is mango. It's quick and easy to make.

Remove the flesh from the mangoes, discarding the stones. Cut the flesh into 1 cm (½ in) dice.

Heat the oil in a frying pan over medium heat and add the mustard seeds. When they begin to pop, add the turmeric, mango, chilli, sugar and 1½ teaspoons salt and stir to combine. Reduce the heat to low and stir for 5 minutes, or until the sugar has completely dissolved.

Remove from heat, allow to cool, then transfer the pickle into sterilized airtight jars (see method, page 216) while the mixture is still hot. Seal immediately and allow to cool to room temperature.

Mango pickle can be stored in the refrigerator for up to 4 weeks after opening.

SERVES 4

Vanilla Rice
50 g (1¾ oz/¼ cup) short-grain rice
500 ml (17 fl oz/2 cups) full-cream (whole) milk
100 ml (3½ fl oz) pouring (whipping) cream
6 green cardamom pods, wrapped in muslin (cheesecloth) and tied into a little bag with kitchen string
50 g (1¾ oz/¼ cup) caster (superfine) sugar
finely grated zest of 1 orange
1 vanilla bean, split lengthways

Syrup
90 g (3¼ oz/¼ cup) honey
200 ml (7 fl oz) strained fresh orange juice
3 green cardamom pods

Chilled Vanilla Rice with Orange and Cardamom Syrup.

In India, rice is used in a lot of the desserts and, being from Yorkshire, I'm a big fan of rice pudding. This recipe is great—the freshness of the orange and the spice of the cardamom are brilliant together. The syrup on the top finishes it off beautifully.

Put the rice and 310 ml (10¾ fl oz/1¼ cups) water in a saucepan over high heat and bring to the boil. Remove from the heat, drain and rinse the rice under cold running water.

Return the rice to a clean saucepan. Add the milk, cream, cardamom, sugar, orange zest and vanilla bean and slowly bring to the boil over medium-high heat. Reduce the heat and simmer for about 45 minutes–1 hour, or until the rice is tender and the liquid has thickened. Remove from the heat, place in a bowl and allow to cool slightly. Cover and refrigerate for at least 4 hours before serving.

To make the syrup, put the honey, orange juice, cardamom and 2 tablespoons water in a saucepan over medium heat. Bring to the boil, then reduce the heat and simmer for 20 minutes, or until the liquid has reduced by half. Pass through a sieve, set aside and refrigerate until needed.

To serve, spoon the vanilla rice into individual bowls and drizzle the syrup over the top.

THE HOLY COW

There are over 200 million cows in India. They're considered sacred for many reasons, one of the main ones being that cows provide people with valuable foods such as milk, yoghurt, butter, cream, ghee and cheese. For many years, one of the first sights visitors had of India was of stray cows lying about or wandering freely on the road.

With increased traffic volume in recent years, cows have become a major headache. In Delhi and other booming cities, they have begun herding cows into safer quarters on the outskirts of the city. Today, you'll only find pockets of Delhi where cows roam freely.

SERVES 6

750 ml (26 fl oz/3 cups) red wine (a spicy shiraz would be good)
200 g (7 oz) honey
250 g (9 oz) caster (superfine) sugar
6 star anise
3 cinnamon sticks
4 cardamom pods
1 vanilla bean, split lengthways, seeds scraped
6 quinces, peeled, cored and cut into quarters
500 g (1 lb 2 oz/2 cups) plain yoghurt, to serve (optional)

Walnut Shortbread
500 g (1 lb 2 oz) unsalted butter, diced
250 g (9 oz) caster (superfine) sugar
700 g (1 lb 9 oz/5 ⅔ cups) plain (all-purpose) flour
250 g (9 oz/2 cups) walnuts, roughly chopped

Poached Spiced Quince with Walnut Shortbread.

Throughout my travels, I found that fruit was used a lot in desserts. In this recipe, I've incorporated the spices that remind me fondly of my journeys through the spice markets.

You can use pears instead of quinces if quinces aren't available. I've added a walnut shortbread to accompany the fruit. You can prepare the shortbread while the fruit is cooking.

Place the wine, honey, sugar, spices, vanilla bean and seeds and 350 ml (12 fl oz) water in a large saucepan, over medium heat. Stir well until the sugar has completely dissolved.

Add the quinces and bring to the boil. Remove from the heat and leave to stand for 20 minutes. Repeat this boiling process another three times; this allows the quince to take on the ruby colour of the wine without overcooking.

Take half of the cooking liquor, discarding the rest, and place in a separate saucepan over high heat. Bring to the boil and cook for 25 minutes, or until the liquid reduces by half and becomes syrupy. Remove from the heat and allow to cool. Refrigerate until ready to serve.

To make the walnut shortbread, preheat the oven to 160°C (315°F/Gas 2–3). Lightly grease a baking tray.

In a mixing bowl, cream together the butter and sugar until pale in colour. Fold in the sifted flour and walnuts and mix to combine well. Roll the dough out on a lightly floured surface to 1.5 cm (⅝ in) thick. Cut the dough into 3 x 10 cm (1 ¼ x 4 in) rectangles and place on the tray. Bake for 12–15 minutes, or until pale golden. Remove from the oven and allow to cool.

Place some quince pieces in each bowl and pour over the syrup. (This can also be gently heated if you prefer.) Serve with the yoghurt if desired, and the walnut shortbread.

This recipe will make more shortbread than you will need to accompany the quince. The shortbread can be stored in an airtight container for 2 weeks.

Rajasthan—A Desert Celebration

There is no better opportunity than a wedding to showcase food in India. Marriages are the backbone of Indian life, bringing communities, castes and families together. Hindus consider it a sacred duty to marry; husband and wife are seen as the two wheels on the chariot of life. Most Indian marriages are still arranged, and the wedding date must be an auspicious one set by astrologers. While filming *Feast*, I was invited to a Hindu wedding. The lucky couple were Pinaji and Priti and the celebrations were to take place in the bride-to-be's hometown of Ghanerao, set in the green belt of Central Rajasthan.

The traditional *mehendi* or henna ceremony takes place the night before the wedding. You could say it's an Indian version of the hen's party, where natural dye is used to paint intricate designs on the bride's hands and feet while women sing traditional wedding songs. As it was Priti's last night at home, she had her favourite dishes cooked for her.

On Pinaji and Priti's wedding day, the din of the wedding procession was heard throughout the tiny township—there were drums, a trumpet and a singer accompanied by a distorted Casio keyboard. The bride was led through the village on horseback adorned with garlands of flowers; a child sat behind her to symbolize innocence. Along the way, there were stops to dance and have a bit of fun. The bride was then blessed and welcomed by her future mother-in-law. After this ritual finished, the horse and band repeated the performance for the groom. As our host Upendra described it, this was a typical village wedding.

I was slightly concerned because the bride and groom didn't appear to be smiling much, but I soon learned that it's traditional for the couple to be seen as serious, while the guests around them do the celebrating. (I think they may have been a wee bit nervous as well.)

After a long photo session with both sides of the family, I thought the big moment had arrived but, no, not quite yet. Pinaji and Priti disappeared in different directions, leaving the guests to enjoy the wedding feast. Customarily, women and children are the first to eat, while the men sit back and talk. There are literally hundreds of dishes that may be served at an Indian wedding, and the cooks know them all off by heart. The wedding feast is served on thalis, which are large round stainless steel trays in which several small bowls are placed. Dal, savoury rice, sweet and sour pickles, deep-fried vegetables, curry, chapati bread and all sorts of sweets were dished out. Waiters will fill up your bowls until you tell them to stop. During dinner, I was feeling a little confused. The intended couple, the Brahmin priest, and immediate

family had moved to the courtyard, where a wedding altar had been set up.

There are seven steps or rounds where promises are made between the bride and groom, to ensure a good marriage. By 2 am, I was ready for bed, but the Brahmin priest and the wedding party were still waiting for the stars to align in accordance with the astrologer's requirements. With all the rituals, processions and astrology, I now understand why Hindu wedding ceremonies take days to complete. Pinaji and Priti were finally married at 3.30 am.

The day after the wedding celebrations we drove on to the whitewashed holy town of Pushkar, one of India's most sacred places. Attracting pilgrims from far and wide, people go to Pushkar with offerings and to bathe in the holy lake—it is said that when Lord Brahma, the creator of the Universe, dropped a lotus flower, it landed in the desert here and a lake magically appeared. Pushkar has over 500 temples (strict vegetarianism forbids even the use of eggs, and alcohol is definitely off the menu) and is a great place to see some of India's colourful Sadhus or holy men who travel around the country living a life of penance and austerity in the hope of achieving enlightenment.

All this changes when the Camel Fair comes to town and the population swells to over 200 000. This annual event on the lunar calendar is also a religious festival, and pilgrims and villagers from all over India set up camp in the dunes. With 50 000 camels and cattle up for sale, it's the largest livestock market in the world. There are hotly contested camel and horse races and even livestock beauty competitions! Indians take great pride in their animals; 550 million farmers rely on these beasts to earn a living.

After the mayhem of the Camel Fair, I enjoyed the peaceful drive to our next filming location, the salt mines of Baap Rin in the desert near Jodphur. Thousands of wells have been bored into the underground salt springs. The water is pumped into these large evaporating ponds, and nature takes its course. As we soon found out, salt harvesting is tough and thirsty work and salt itself is steeped in history.

The ancient Greeks swapped salt for slaves, giving us the expression 'not worth his salt'. The word 'salary' comes from the salt rations given to Roman soldiers. When the British Raj ruled India, they introduced a salt tax that essentially made it illegal to sell or produce salt. Even the poorest workers who collected salt from the coastal areas were forced to buy it.

It was this particular indignity that Gandhi used as a focus for the 'Quit India' campaign,

climaxing with the famous non-violent Salt March in 1930—23 days and 384 kilometres (240 miles) later, Gandhi and his fellow protesters arrived on the coast to produce salt illegally. As a result, Gandhi was imprisoned. However, the 'Quit India' movement, that began with salt and freedom as its focus, eventually gained India the rights to both.

It was on the way to the salt mines that I was introduced to the pleasures of a crunchy snack known as vadas. In the main street of a dusty non-descript town we stopped near two stalls set up next to each other, both doing a roaring trade. Apparently they are famous for their vadas, which are made from ground wild lentils that are soaked in water before being mixed with cumin and coriander seeds, garlic, salt and chilli. This mixture is then flicked into a pan of hot, bubbling coconut oil and cooked until crisp and golden. There was great showmanship in the way these vadas were being made, and I was mesmerized by the rhythm of it all. Deep-fried green chillies were served as an accompaniment, making the eating experience a memorable one (see recipe, page 79).

As we drove along, we saw a procession of women with clay or brass pots perched upon their heads, making their daily journey to the nearest well. For these women, a visit to the well means more than just fetching water. It's a chance to meet and talk to other women, without the company of men, and an opportunity to escape the monotony of household chores. Stock are watered, and bodies and clothes are washed and cleaned.

My Rajasthan guide and good friend, Gaju, is a volunteer with Native Planet, a non-profit organisation that works with tribal groups to preserve their cultural identity. He invited me to experience a Bishnoi village first-hand.

We journeyed three hours by road and another two hours by camel cart. While swaying along the sandy tracks, I couldn't help wondering what type of person could make a life in such a harsh environment. The Bishnoi are a proud Rajasthani tribal group who practise a religion that is an offshoot of Hinduism. The main difference is the Bishnoi have no castes; they consider all people equal and most of the twenty-nine religious principles focus on a deep respect for nature. They're vegetarian and will not kill any living creature or even cut down trees. Only dead wood can be collected and used.

The homes of the Bishnoi are very simple, the floors and walls are constructed from mud and straw that is regularly covered with fresh layers of cow dung. The dung has disinfectant and insect repellent qualities, while the clay fills the inevitable cracks created by the dry conditions. Most of these isolated villages and houses have no power; in fact, I could see no sign of modern technology and it was easy to imagine that nothing has changed in these villages for centuries. Water is obviously a precious commodity here—dishes are cleaned with dry sand only, and clothes and bodies are washed in the salty, undrinkable water from the village bore wells.

The village was celebrating the arranged marriage of two twelve-year-olds. The couple won't meet until they are considered mature enough to live together as a married couple. In the meantime, they'll continue living at home with their own families. It may lack romance, but the purpose of marriage here is to forge bonds that will continue to keep these communities strong.

For Bishnoi women, jewellery is their only real possession, and what a woman receives as part of her wedding dowry appears to be worn in its entirety. Every conceivable place where jewellery could be worn has been adorned—there are toe and finger rings, earrings, anklets, necklaces, armbands, bracelets, forehead ornaments and the gold nose rings worn by all married women of this tribe. Turbans are a statement of religion or tribe. Ten metres of cloth is tied in a myriad of styles, each revealing something about the man. Bishnoi men wear white as a symbol of modesty and equality.

Visiting the Bishnoi people was a truly memorable experience. Their food was basic—lentils and vegetables were almost always served, with bread being the staple of each meal. But it was the ritual of preparing and eating that gave me the most valuable insight into their daily life and I was able to observe a culture that is respectful of each person and the Earth.

SERVES 4 AS A SNACK

125 g (4½ oz/½ cup) moong dal (see glossary)
125 g (4½ oz/½ cup) urad dal (see glossary)
1 brown onion, finely chopped
2 teaspoons ground coriander
1 long green chilli, finely chopped
1 teaspoon freshly grated ginger
¼ teaspoon bicarbonate of soda (baking soda)
vegetable oil, for frying
4 whole long green chillies, to garnish

Lentil Vadas. When we were driving across Rajasthan, Gaju, our amazing friend and guide, asked the driver to stop so he could get us a roadside snack. He got back on the bus holding small parcels wrapped in newspaper.

When I unwrapped mine, what was inside looked like little chicken nuggets with deep-fried green chillies as a garnish. I put the first vada in my mouth and, before I knew it, I was wolfing them down. We only got a few kilometres further down the road before there was a unanimous vote to turn back for more.

Soak the moong dal and urad dal in cold water for 2–3 hours. Drain and rinse well. Blend or grind into a coarse paste in a food processor or using a mortar and pestle.

Transfer to a bowl and add the onion, coriander, chilli, ginger, bicarbonate of soda and 1 teaspoon salt. Mix well and allow to stand for 15 minutes.

Heat the oil in a wok or large heavy-based saucepan to 180°C (350°F), or until a cube of bread dropped into the oil browns in 15 seconds.

Drop teaspoonfuls of the mixture into the hot oil, in batches, and deep-fry for 5 minutes each, or until golden brown. Remove with a slotted spoon and drain on paper towel.

Pierce the whole chillies three times each with the point of a sharp knife and deep-fry for about 2–3 minutes, or until the skins start to bubble.

Serve the lentil vadas hot as a snack with the deep-fried chillies to garnish.

MAKES 6

1 kg (2 lb 4 oz/6⅔ cups) wholemeal (wholewheat) flour, plus extra, for dusting
1 tablespoon vegetable oil

Chapatis. Bread is a staple throughout India, and is served with every meal. I remember eating in Delhi's Gurudwara Bangla Sahib Sikh Temple. It's a place where anyone can come to eat, and I was told they serve up to 70 000 meals per day. The organization in the kitchen was outstanding. The food was simple but tasted very good. Groups of school children and a team of volunteers sat on mats rolling out the chapati. There was also an ingenious chapati-making machine that churned out over a thousand an hour; the ingredients were placed in at one end and cooked chapati came out the other. All the ingredients were donated by the local Sikh community.

Sift the flour into a mixing bowl and add the sifted husks back in. Make a well in the centre and add the oil, ½ teaspoon salt and 750 ml (26 fl oz/3 cups) water. Gently fold the mixture together until a soft dough forms. Set aside for 10–15 minutes, covered with a damp tea towel (dish towel).

Dust your hands with a little flour and form the mixture into six even-sized balls (about the size of a tennis ball). Flatten slightly with your hand, then, using a rolling pin, roll them out on a lightly floured bench until they are 5 mm (¼ in) thick and 10 cm (4 in) in diameter.

Heat a non-stick frying pan over medium heat. Working one at a time, gently dry-fry each chapati on both sides for 2–3 minutes, or until a deep golden brown.

Serve the chapatis immediately with any meal as a bread option.

MAKES 200 G (7 OZ/1½ CUPS)

1 tablespoon vegetable oil
¼ teaspoon nigella seeds (see glossary)
¼ teaspoon brown mustard seeds
¼ teaspoon ground cumin
¼ teaspoon ground ginger
¼ teaspoon chilli powder
500 g (1 lb 2 oz) large tomatoes, peeled (see method, page 215) and roughly diced
1 brown onion, finely diced
115 g (4 oz/½ cup) firmly packed soft brown sugar

Indian Tomato Chutney. Chutneys and pickles are common across India and no Indian meal would be complete without them. Chutney comes from the Hindu word 'chatni' meaning 'for licking', as in relishing an appetizing flavour for the taste. Chutneys are usually eaten in small amounts and add flavour to a meal. Chutneys are very versatile and go with everything including fish, meats, curries and poppadoms.

Heat the oil in a heavy-based saucepan over medium heat and add the nigella and mustard seeds. When they start to pop, add the cumin, ginger and chilli. Mix well and cook for about 2 minutes to allow the flavour of the spices to deepen as they release their aromas.

Reduce the heat, add the tomato and onion and cook for about 5 minutes, or until the onion is transparent. Add ½ teaspoon salt, then stir in the sugar. Simmer gently for a further 10 minutes, stirring occasionally until the mixture thickens.

Remove from the heat. Pour the hot chutney into a sterilized airtight jar (see method, page 216) and seal. You can store the chutney for up to 4 weeks in the refrigerator once opened.

MAKES 8

400 g (14 oz) all-purpose potatoes, peeled, boiled and roughly mashed
2 long green chillies, finely chopped
1 small brown onion, finely chopped
2 large handfuls coriander (cilantro) leaves, finely chopped
pinch of ajowan seeds (see glossary)
100 g (3½ oz) butter, softened
300 g (10½ oz/2 cups) wholemeal (whole-wheat) flour
1 tablespoon vegetable oil

Parathas—Potato-stuffed Unleavened Bread. I loved the breads in India—there is so much variety and flavour. This recipe is one of my favourites. The potato filling gives it a unique flavour.

In a mixing bowl, mix the potato, chilli, onion, coriander, ajowan seeds and ½ teaspoon salt with 50 g (1¾ oz) of the butter.

Place the flour in a separate bowl with 150 ml (5 fl oz) warm water and mix for 5 minutes, or until a pliable dough forms.

Divide the dough into 8 even-sized balls and cover with a damp tea towel (dish towel) to prevent them from drying out.

Working with one ball at a time, slightly flatten it into a bowl shape in the palm of your hand. Place 1 tablespoon of the potato mixture, into the centre of the dough and bring the edges together in a half-moon shape. Pinch the edges to seal, making sure that all of the filling is covered.

Lightly dust the bench with flour. Roll each dough out into a disc with a 12 cm (4½ in) diameter and 1 cm (½ in) thick. Repeat with the remaining seven balls.

Heat the oil in a non-stick frying pan over medium heat, add a teaspoon of butter and fry the parathas one by one, for about 1 minute on each side, or until light golden brown, adding extra butter as needed.

Parathas taste great served with raita (see glossary), mango pickle (see recipe, page 68) or mustard pickle (see recipe, page 66).

SERVES 4

50 g (1¾ oz) moong dal (see glossary)
100 g (3½ oz) red lentils
60 ml (2 fl oz/¼ cup) vegetable oil
1 brown onion, finely chopped
½ teaspoon ground ginger
¼ teaspoon crushed garlic
¼ teaspoon ground turmeric
½ teaspoon cumin seeds
¼ teaspoon chopped long red chillies
3 medium green chillies, seeds removed and thinly sliced
2 large tomatoes, peeled (see method, page 215) and diced
1 handful coriander (cilantro) leaves, roughly chopped

Dal. Dal is a mainstay throughout India, Africa and the Middle East. Lentils are the key ingredient. In India, dal is a popular staple as it's cheap, vegetarian (most people in India are vegetarian) and very nutritious. You find dal everywhere you go—the tastes vary slightly, depending on the region, as everyone has their own recipe.

Wash the dal and lentils well, removing any grit. Place in a deep saucepan, cover with 1 litre (35 fl oz/4 cups) water and add a pinch of salt. Bring almost to the boil over medium heat, then reduce the heat and simmer gently, stirring frequently, for approximately15–20 minutes, or until the liquid is absorbed and the dal and lentils are soft.

Meanwhile, heat the oil in a heavy-based frying pan over medium heat and sauté the onion for 10 minutes, or until golden brown. Add the ginger, garlic, turmeric, cumin seeds, chilli, tomato and coriander. Mix well and cook gently for about 5 minutes, or until the tomato is softened. Stir into the dal mixture and season, to taste.

Serve with Basmati Rice (see recipe, page 214) and Chapatis (see recipe, page 80).

SERVES 4 AS A SIDE DISH

400 g (14 oz) okra
8 tablespoons mustard oil (see glossary)
2 brown onions, finely chopped
1 tablespoon hot mustard

Curried Okra. Okra (or ladies' fingers) is very popular on menus across India. I had eaten okra before in other countries, but hadn't really enjoyed it. Tasting okra cooked Indian-style changed my mind about this vegetable.

Wash the okra well. Cut into 3 cm (1¼ in) lengths, discarding the stalks.

Heat the mustard oil in a wok or large frying pan over medium heat, then add the onion and cook for about 8–10 minutes, or until golden brown.

Add the okra and fry for 2–3 minutes. Stir in the mustard paste and season with 1 teaspoon salt. Sauté for a further 5 minutes, or until the okra is tender. Serve immediately. Curried okra tastes great served with Crisp Spiced Fish (see recipe, page 47).

SERVES 4

1.8–2 kg (4 lb–4 lb 8 oz) leg of lamb on the bone
4 tablespoons vegetable oil
4 garlic cloves, crushed
250 g (9 oz/1 cup) plain yoghurt
1 tablespoon garam masala (see recipe, page 60)
1 ½ teaspoons freshly grated ginger
¼ teaspoon hot chilli powder
small pinch saffron threads

Marinated Roast Leg of Lamb. I am told that there are many different versions of this recipe in India, some of which have been eaten by emperors and maharajas. This particular version has been simplified for the home cook. You can't go wrong with lamb, and this marinade makes it very special.

Using a small paring knife, pierce the flesh of the lamb all over. In a bowl, stir the remaining ingredients with ½ teaspoon salt and mix well.

Place the lamb in a deep, large, non-metallic dish and coat all over with the marinade. Cover with plastic wrap and refrigerate for at least 3 hours.

Preheat the oven to 180°C (350°F/Gas 4). Transfer the lamb to a roasting tin, cover with foil and slowly roast the lamb for about 2 hours, or until the meat is tender.

Remove the foil, baste the lamb with the juices and cook for a further 15 minutes to allow the outside to brown slightly. Remove from the oven and leave to rest in a warm place for 10 minutes before carving.

This lamb roast is best served with a simple green salad and Chapatis (see recipe, page 80); the flavour is in the lamb and it should be enjoyed to its fullest.

SERVES 4

2 kg (4 lb 8 oz) whole chicken
90 g (3¼ oz/⅓ cup) plain yoghurt
100 ml (3½ fl oz) pouring (whipping) cream
1½ teaspoons garam masala (see recipe, page 60)
2 tablespoons paprika
1 teaspoon hot chilli powder
1 teaspoon ground cumin
½ teaspoon ground turmeric
2 tablespoons lemon juice
2 tablespoons vegetable oil
1 tablespoon tomato paste (concentrated purée)
5 garlic cloves, crushed
2½ teaspoons finely grated fresh ginger

A Whole Tandoori Chicken. Of course a traditional tandoor oven is the best way to cook this dish, but I can assure you that this recipe will also taste fantastic when you cook it at home. You need to start this recipe the day before you wish to serve it to allow the chicken to marinate overnight.

Pierce the chicken all over with a metal skewer, inserting the skewer about 2 cm (¾ in) deep.

Place the remaining ingredients in a bowl with 1 teaspoon salt and mix well to combine. Rub the marinade all over the chicken, making sure you coat all sides. Place the chicken in a large non-metallic dish, cover with plastic wrap and refrigerate overnight.

Preheat the oven to 180°C (350°F/Gas 4). Place the chicken in a roasting tin. Cook for 1½ hours, or until the juices run clear when the thickest part of the thigh is pierced with a sharp knife. Baste the chicken with the pan juices a few times during cooking.

Remove from the oven, cover lightly with foil and allow to rest for about 20 minutes before carving. Serve with Aloo Gobhi (see recipe, page 61) and your favourite bread.

SERVES 2

410 g (14½ oz/1⅔ cups) plain yoghurt
250 ml (9 fl oz/1 cup) full-cream (whole) milk
80 ml (2½ fl oz/⅓ cup) pouring (whipping) cream
2 tablespoons caster (superfine) sugar
¼ teaspoon natural vanilla extract
2 bananas
ice, to serve
freshly grated nutmeg, to serve

Vanilla and Banana Lassi. Besides chai, lassi would have to be the most popular drink of the Indian people. A lassi is made in one of two ways—either sweet or salty. It's a wonderfully refreshing drink in hot weather, and is also used after meals to aid digestion.

Place everything except the ice and nutmeg in a blender and blend until smooth.

Half-fill two tall glasses with ice and pour in the lassi. Sprinkle the nutmeg on top, to serve.

SERVES 4

100 ml (3½ fl oz) pouring (whipping) cream
200 ml (7 fl oz) full-cream (whole) milk
310 g (11 oz/1¼ cups) plain yoghurt
¼ teaspoon natural vanilla extract
3 teaspoons caster (superfine) sugar
2 tablespoons rosewater
ice, to serve
freshly grated nutmeg, to serve
pinch saffron threads, to serve (optional)

Vanilla Lassi with Rosewater. There are many different variations and flavours for lassis including vanilla, mango, cardamom, black pepper and mint. Here is a version I particularly enjoy, flavoured with rosewater.

Blend all the ingredients, except the ice and nutmeg, in a blender until smooth.

Half-fill two tall glasses with ice and pour in the lassi. Sprinkle the nutmeg and saffron (if using) on top, to serve.

MOROCCO

Morocco

From the coastline of Essaouira, across the High Atlas Mountains to Marrakech, Fez and Casablanca and all the quirky villages in between, Morocco is a land of true colour and beauty

If you want to experience the authentic life of the locals a visit to the souks, or markets, is essential. These are located in the smallest villages (some with their own parking lot for donkeys) and major cities of Morocco. Moroccans are very proud people and are also proud of the food they serve. Experiencing this first-hand gave me a great appreciation for their food customs—the important role they play in daily family life and also as part of religious traditions. Nowhere is this love of food more apparent than at the souks, which contain an abundance of spice shops and local produce. It quickly became obvious to me that every Moroccan family has their own version of regional dishes that they pass down the female line from one generation to the next. Not all of these recipes are written down, but once made, they can offer a unique insight into some of the most appetizing cuisine in the world.

As was typical of my journeys for *Feast Bazaar*, I found in Morocco that the best eating experiences were to be had in the small villages. Here I found recipes that were steeped in history and made from the heart, with some of the freshest organic ingredients on offer. The traditions of the Berbers have stood the test of time. They eat what they farm and follow the seasons. I was lucky enough to spend a day on a Berber farm where I experienced couscous being made from scratch—a unique and unforgettable experience with a flavour to match. I hope the recipes that follow will give you an inkling of the spectacular diversity of Moroccan food and flavours that are just one part of this remarkable country.

Marrakech

The legendary city of Marrakech was once called the last oasis. Today it still lures travellers from around the globe. Marrakech has always been caught between two worlds. At its heart is the medina, or old city, surrounded by a wall that stretches for 12 kilometres (7 miles). Here it's easy to think you've travelled back in time.

In the nouvelle areas, you can find all the gadgets and accessories of present-day Europe. Most people are trilingual, speaking Berber, Arabic and French. Originally a Berber stronghold, the very name Marrakech conjures up tales of Arabian nights and rose-scented gardens. Featured in many romantic tales and songs, Marrakech also has a rich history as a magnetic trading centre.

For a thousand years, caravans arrived every day laden with the rare, the strange and the precious. Now jumbo jets have replaced camels, bringing a whole new trade: Europeans in search of the exotic arrive in their hundreds every day. In the 1970s came the hippies; now they're returning as cashed-up tourists looking for a piece of magic.

Most souks date back over 1200 years. Stalls sell everything from silver teapots, long loose-hooded garments worn in Muslim countries known as *jellabas*, sweets, dyed fabrics, trinkets and leather goods to huge mounds of fresh herbs, such as mint.

You can't come to Marrakech without visiting Djemaa el-Fna, the busiest square in Africa. During the day, the square is filled with small stalls offering charms, potions, jewellery and henna tattoos, or stacked high with carpets, slippers and lanterns. You'll also find loads of delicatessens, Middle Eastern-style.

It wasn't that long ago that slaves from sub-Saharan Africa were sold off in their tens of thousands in this very place. Now acrobats, fortune-tellers, fire-eaters, snake charmers and faith healers try to earn a little baksheesh. *Gnawas*, a tribe of former slaves, roam around the square singing and playing drums. Crowds form around mock boxing matches featuring juvenile opponents. Dream merchants, usually sitting beneath large umbrellas, are very popular with the locals; and then there are the storytellers—the oral tradition is still very important here.

Each evening, as the sun dips beside the Koutoubia Mosque, the square magically transforms into one of the world's largest open-air kitchens. Signs are hung, coloured lights strung up, lamps and braziers lit, and the stage is set for a night of Moroccan magic. The air is full of the pungent aroma of baked bulls' testicles, snails, steamed sheep's head, mysterious sausages and calves' hooves, plus dishes to suit the less adventurous.

An influx of traders into Morocco over time has seen an introduction of various exotic foods. Over time, Moroccans have mixed and adapted this palette of flavours to their own taste, and it's this blend of different influences that has made Moroccan cuisine so universally popular.

In Morocco, bread is the cornerstone of every meal and in almost every street you can smell the delicious aroma of freshly baked bread cooked in the neighbourhood's wood-fired ovens. The bakeries also double as meeting places, and are hives of activity. Bread dough arrives on trays each day from the surrounding households, delivered by women and children. Each batch is baked for a small fee and the pace never lets up.

Marrakech is timeless; it floats magically between the present and the distant past. It is both intoxicating and exotic and its magnetism will, I'm sure, lure me back again one day.

حسن
3
Hassane
3
40

MAKES 250 ML (9 FL OZ/1 CUP)

1 handful coriander (cilantro) leaves
2 garlic cloves, peeled
2 handfuls flat-leaf (Italian) parsley
1½ teaspoons ground cumin
1½ teaspoons ground coriander
1½ teaspoons ground paprika
1 small red chilli, seeds removed
2½ tablespoons lemon juice
1½ tablespoons lime juice
125 ml (4 fl oz/½ cup) olive oil

Chermoula. Chermoula is a marinade that is often used with fish, but also works wonderfully with lamb and chicken. It can be used as a dipping sauce with bread. In my restaurant I use it with spatchcock.

Chermoula is made with typical North African ingredients, and is hot to taste. Make sure you marinate the meat in the refrigerator for at least 24 hours before cooking.

Put all the ingredients in a food processor or a mortar and pestle and blend or grind to a smooth paste. Add 1 teaspoon salt and mix to thoroughly combine.

Store in an airtight container in the refrigerator until ready to use. Chermoula will keep for about 1 week stored in the refrigerator.

SERVES 6

5 oranges
20 black olives
1 red onion, sliced into rings
2½ tablespoons lemon juice
3 tablespoons argan oil (see glossary) or olive oil
½ teaspoon ground cumin
½ teaspoon paprika
pinch of ground chilli powder
1 handful flat-leaf (Italian) parsley, chopped

Olive, Orange and Onion Salad. This salad has a great mix of refreshing flavours. The acidity works well alongside the heaviness and richness of meat dishes. It is best made with argan oil, if you can get it, which has a unique flavour.

Peel the oranges and make sure you remove any pith, then cut each orange into eight wedges. Lay the oranges on a large flat plate, then scatter over the olives and red onion.

To make the dressing, mix the lemon juice, argan oil, cumin, paprika, chilli powder and parsley. Season, to taste, and drizzle over the salad, to serve.

SERVES 4 AS A SIDE DISH

1 cauliflower, cut into small florets
2 garlic cloves, crushed
3 tablespoons tahini
1 teaspoon ground cumin
finely grated zest of 1 lemon
2½ tablespoons lemon juice
few drops of Tabasco sauce
sea salt and freshly ground black pepper, to taste
ground sumac, to garnish

Middle Eastern Cauliflower and Tahini. This dish is often served with dips as an entrée or mezze. I am a big fan of cauliflower, and with the tahini this recipe brings out its wonderful texture and flavour.

Cook the cauliflower in a saucepan of boiling salted water for 6 minutes, or until tender. Drain and refresh in cold water. Drain again and set aside.

Mix the garlic, tahini, cumin, lemon zest, lemon juice and Tabasco in a bowl. Add a little water, if necessary, to loosen the paste so it will easily coat the cauliflower florets. Add the cauliflower and mix well until the florets are well coated. Season to taste and refrigerate until needed. Sprinkle with sumac, to serve.

This dish can also be served warm. If you wish to do so, mix the tahini mixture with the cauliflower as soon as it is cooked.

SERVES 6

1 kg (2 lb 4 oz) eggplant (aubergine)
4 tablespoons olive oil
500 g (1 lb 2 oz) tomatoes, peeled (see method, page 215) and chopped
5 garlic cloves, finely chopped
2½ tablespoons lemon juice
½ teaspoon paprika
pinch of chilli powder, to taste
1 teaspoon ground cumin
1 handful flat-leaf (Italian) parsley, chopped
1 handful coriander (cilantro) leaves, chopped
sea salt and freshly ground black pepper, to taste
20 black olives

Mashed Eggplant and Tomato Salad. I had this salad quite a few times in Morocco. This dish is great as a snack with some good bread and a glass of wine.

Preheat the oven to 240°C (475°F/Gas 8).

Prick the eggplants a few times to prevent them bursting while in the oven. Wrap each eggplant in foil, place on a roasting tray and bake for about 45 minutes, or until they feel very soft. Remove from the heat and allow to cool.

Peel each eggplant and discard the skin. Place the flesh into a strainer and gently press out as much of the juice as possible. Finely chop the remaining pulp.

Heat the oil in a frying pan over medium heat and cook the tomatoes and garlic with 1 teaspoon salt. Bring to the boil, then reduce the heat and simmer for 15–20 minutes, or until thickened. Remove from the heat and allow to cool.

Mix the tomato and eggplant together in a bowl. Add the lemon juice, spices and herbs and stir thoroughly to coat. Season with sea salt and freshly ground black pepper, to taste. Serve in a large serving dish and garnish with the olives.

SERVES 4

1.5 kg (3 lb 5 oz) whole chicken
80 ml (2½ fl oz/⅓ cup) olive oil
2 brown onions, finely chopped
3 garlic cloves, finely chopped
finely chopped zest of 1 lemon
2 red capsicums (peppers), seeded and diced
1 green capsicum (pepper), seeded and diced
1 small red chilli, seeded and thinly sliced
1 tablespoon finely chopped rosemary leaves
1 bay leaf
125 ml (4 fl oz/½ cup) dry white wine
70 g (2½ oz) tomato paste (concentrated purée)
3 roma (plum) tomatoes, peeled (see method, page 215), seeded and chopped
420 ml (14½ fl oz/1⅔ cups) chicken stock
100 g (3½ oz/¼ cup) honey
100 g (3½ oz) pitted black olives
salt and freshly ground black pepper, to taste
1 handful mint leaves, finely chopped

Sauté of Chicken with Honey and Mint.

Chicken dishes like this one were very popular throughout Morocco and upon tasting it I could see why. The honey and fresh mint complement the chicken very well.

Preheat the oven to 220°C (425°F/Gas 7). Cut the chicken into 8 pieces (see method, page 214).

Heat the oil in a heavy-based saucepan over medium–high heat. Add the chicken and cook for 5 minutes, turning to seal on all sides. Remove from the pan and set aside.

Add the onion, garlic, lemon zest, capsicums and chilli to the pan with the rosemary, bay leaf and white wine. Bring to the boil and cook for 5 minutes, or until the liquid has reduced by half. Add the tomato paste and chopped tomatoes, pour in the chicken stock and honey and bring to the boil. Skim off any impurities that rise to the surface.

Add the chicken and olives to the pan, cover, and place in the oven for about 45 minutes, or until the chicken is cooked through and tender.

Check the seasoning, add the chopped mint and serve immediately.

SERVES 4

Shakshouka Sauce
100 ml (3½ fl oz) olive oil
1 brown onion, thinly sliced
4 garlic cloves, crushed
750 g (1 lb 10 oz) tomatoes, peeled (see method, page 215) and finely chopped
750 g (1 lb 10 oz) green capsicums (peppers), grilled, peeled (see method, page 215) and finely chopped
½ teaspoon mild chilli powder
½ teaspoon ground cumin
½ teaspoon ground allspice
1 handful flat-leaf (Italian) parsley, finely chopped
1 handful coriander (cilantro) leaves, finely chopped

60 ml (2 fl oz/¼ cup) olive oil, plus extra, for frying
7 tablespoons black peppercorns, cracked
2 tablespoons Dijon mustard
1 tablespoon soy sauce
4 swordfish steaks, about 140 g (5 oz) each
sea salt, to taste
2 limes, cut in half, to serve

Swordfish with Shakshouka. I grew up eating basic, everyday fish like cod and haddock. Swordfish was the first, shall I say, 'different' fish that I tasted. It has such a meaty texture, and a remarkable flavour. Shakshouka sauce works really well with grilled fish or roast meats.

To make the shakshouka sauce, heat the oil in a frying pan over low heat and gently fry the onion, garlic, tomato and capsicum for about 30 minutes, or until softened. Add the chilli, cumin and allspice. Season with salt and pepper and cook for a further 10 minutes to allow the flavours to infuse. Finally, stir through the chopped herbs. Remove from the heat and keep warm until ready to serve.

To prepare the swordfish, mix the olive oil, peppercorns, mustard and soy sauce in a small bowl. Coat each of the swordfish steaks well and season with sea salt, to taste.

Heat a little extra olive oil in a non-stick frying pan over high heat. Quickly fry the swordfish for 1 minute on each side, or until seared well—the swordfish should still be rare.

Spoon about 3 tablespoons of the shakshouka sauce evenly over the swordfish on each plate. Serve immediately with half a lime for your guests to squeeze over the top.

SERVES 4

60 ml (2 fl oz/¼ cup) olive oil
2 onions, finely chopped
3 garlic cloves, crushed
pinch of saffron threads
½ teaspoon ground ginger
250 ml (9 fl oz/1 cup) chicken stock
1.8 kg (4 lb) whole chicken, cut into 8 pieces (see method page 214)
sea salt and freshly ground black pepper, to taste
1 tablespoon lemon juice
1 handful coriander (cilantro) leaves, chopped
1 handful flat-leaf (Italian) parsley, chopped
peel of 1 whole preserved lemon, pith removed, rinsed well and roughly chopped
16 green olives
400 g (14 oz) tin artichokes in brine, cut into quarters and rinsed well

Tagine of Chicken with Artichokes, Preserved Lemon and Olives. I tasted my first tagine in Morocco, and you can't get a more authentic food experience than that! I have used tinned artichokes in brine for this recipe, but you can use fresh when they are in season, provided they are cooked first.

In a tagine or flameproof casserole dish that is large enough to hold all the chicken pieces in one even layer, heat the olive oil over low heat. Add the onions and sauté, stirring, for about 8–10 minutes, or until soft. Add the garlic, saffron and ginger and stir to coat. Add the chicken pieces and chicken stock and season to taste. Bring to the boil over medium–high heat, then reduce the heat and simmer for 20 minutes, turning the chicken a couple of times. Add a little more stock if it becomes too dry. Remove the chicken breasts, set aside and keep warm.

Continue to cook the rest of the chicken for about 20 minutes, or until tender, then return the breasts to the tagine. Add the lemon juice, herbs, preserved lemon and olives. Simmer for about 5–8 minutes, or until the sauce thickens slightly. Stir in the artichokes and continue to cook for 2 minutes further, to heat through. Season to taste and serve immediately with Moroccan Bread (see recipe, page 137).

Note: If your tagine is not used frequently you will need to season it before cooking (see method, page 216).

SERVES 4

100 ml (3½ fl oz) olive oil
4 duck breasts, skin on
3 brown onions, thinly sliced
3 garlic cloves, crushed
1 litre (35 fl oz/4 cups) chicken stock
2 teaspoons ground cinnamon
½ teaspoon saffron threads
salt and freshly ground black pepper, to taste
4 firm fresh peaches, cut into 6 wedges, stones removed
1 bunch coriander (cilantro) leaves, roughly chopped

Duck and Peach Tagine. For this dish, you need to cook the duck slowly in the pan to allow the fat to cook out. If fresh peaches are not available, you can substitute dried ones, but you will need to soak them in warm water before use.

Heat a little olive oil in a frying pan over a low heat. Add the duck breasts to the pan and cook slowly for about 3 minutes, skin side down, or until they are a deep golden brown. Turn over and cook for a further 1–2 minutes. Remove from the pan and set aside.

Add the onions and garlic to the pan and cook over medium heat for 10 minutes, or until lightly browned. Remove from the heat and set aside.

Slice each duck breast crossways into six pieces. Put the duck, onions and garlic into a tagine or flameproof casserole dish with a lid. Pour in the stock and add the cinnamon and saffron, stirring to combine. Season to taste.

Cover the tagine and cook over low heat for about 40 minutes, or until the duck is tender and the sauce has thickened slightly. Check the level of stock during cooking and add more if the dish becomes too dry. Add the peaches and cook for a further 10 minutes, or until softened but not falling apart. Stir through the chopped coriander and serve immediately with Couscous (see recipe, page 214).

Note: If your tagine is not used frequently you will need to season it before cooking (see method, page 216)

SERVES 6

9 granny smith apples, peeled and thinly sliced
30 g (1 oz) butter
60 g (2¼ oz) caster (superfine) sugar
12 dried figs, soaked in warm water until plump, drained and thinly sliced
20 sheets filo pastry
1 egg, lightly beaten
icing (confectioner's) sugar, to garnish
ground cinnamon, to garnish

Apple and Fig Bastilla. Dar Fez restaurant in Marrakech was where I first tried pigeon bastilla—the flavours were wonderful. Here I have used the principles and traditional flavours of a bastilla to create a dessert using apples and figs. It's a dish that can be made all year round. If you are lucky enough to have fresh seasonal figs then it will taste even better.

Preheat the oven to 180°C (350°F/Gas 4). Line a baking tray with baking paper.

Put the butter, apples and sugar in a large frying pan over medium heat. Cook for 5 minutes, or until the apples are tender. Remove from the heat, drain off any juice and discard. Set aside and allow to cool.

Place 5 sheets of pastry in the bottom of a bowl with a 20 cm (8 in) diameter and about 5 cm (2 in) deep. Leave the pastry to overhang the edge—this will later be used to wrap and cover the bastilla.

Spread a thin layer of apple over the pastry base, followed by a layer of fig. Press down gently and cover with 2 layers of filo which have been cut to fit snugly inside the bowl.

Repeat this layering with the apple, figs and pastry four more times, finishing with 5 sheets of pastry that have been cut to fit the bowl. Finally, fold over the overhanging pastry from the original base layer and seal. Turn out the bastilla and invert onto the prepared tray so the base is now the top.

Brush all over with the beaten egg. Place in the oven and bake for 15–20 minutes, or until golden brown. Remove from the oven, dust liberally with icing sugar and cinnamon and serve immediately.

Essaouira

Essaouira is a small coastal town on the Atlantic coast of Morocco. It has been invaded many times throughout history, beginning with the Phoenicians around 1200 BC.

The town itself was a plunderers' paradise up until 1760, when a Frenchman re-designed the impressive fortress that until then had failed to protect the port. Today, it is still armed with the original Portuguese and Spanish bronze cannons, although in recent decades the only invaders have come armed with guitars, cameras and credit cards.

Essaouira's local economy depends on the tourist trade. Since it's only a few hours away by plane from Europe, the French, Spanish and English arrive in their thousands. The annual music festival and the souks full of bargain-priced trinkets, wooden and leather goods, ceramics and antiques are all key attractions. The famous wind also makes it a natural setting for the Kiteboard World Cup.

Which all goes some way towards explaining why Essaouira is the most liberal town in Morocco, and a place where you can experience the best of Eastern and Western cultures. Jimi Hendrix was a constant visitor during his short life. Many other famous artists, writers and musicians blew in through the 1970s, turning it into a popular stop on the international hippy trail. It's also been the backdrop for many major films by directors, including Orson Welles and Ridley Scott.

Hippies and Hollywood aside, Essaouira has always been a fishing port—in fact, one of the most important in all of Africa. The main catch is sardines; Morocco is now the largest global producer.

The fishermen of Essaouira have been going to sea in the same small wooden boats for generations. The main difference now is that oars have been replaced by small outboard motors. However, the traditional boat-building methods are still used.

You could spend all day simply walking around the port watching what goes on. There are the trademark blue boats, tethered together, riding the rhythm of the tide. And the dinosaur-like, massive wooden skeletons of the larger deep-water boats. There's the constant departure and arrival of the fishermen with their hard-earned catch, shadowed by the usual flock of screeching gulls.

One of the greatest experiences to be had in Essaouira is to get completely lost in the maze of souks—a warren of fish markets, spice shops and fruit and vegetable stalls. There are many tiny alleys where caged chickens, ducks, doves and rabbits await their inevitable fate.

Unlike India, where a meat stall is hard to find, meat is a prime source of protein in Morocco. Butchers' stalls with fresh carcasses hanging out front are found on nearly every street corner. Similarly, the souks offer an array of produce, with farmers from surrounding villages setting up stalls with fresh vegetables, live rabbits, chicken and ducks. The harbour is filled with stalls selling all manner of seafood fresh off the boat and there are many examples of local restaurants featuring much of this seafood, especially sardines, which are a popular favourite. Like much of the seafood, these recipes are kept simple to relish the natural flavours of the sea, and the sardines are often grilled and served with fresh lemon and local harissa.

For me, Essaouira is both easygoing and exciting—an obvious inspiration for both artists and plunderers alike. I can understand why it's attracted so many invaders and visitors over the centuries. As it turned out, Essaouira wasn't what I expected; it was so much more.

SERVES 6

12 fresh sardines, scaled, gutted and left whole (ask your fishmonger to do this for you)
olive oil, for brushing
sea salt and freshly ground black pepper, to taste
harissa, to serve (see recipe, pages 214–15)
lemon wedges, to serve

Grilled Sardines with Harissa. Seeing all the sardines coming in daily to the port in Essaouira was an awesome sight. Eating the catch of the day was even more tempting. The flavours of fresh sardines go wonderfully with tomato, while harissa gives it a spicy twist.

Preheat a barbecue hotplate or grill (broiler) to high.

Brush the sardines with olive oil and season well. Cook for about 3–4 minutes on each side—they should be cooked through and the skin slightly charred.

Serve with harissa and lemon wedges. Grilled sardines also taste great with Moroccan Tomato and Cucumber Salad (see recipe, page 138).

SERVES 4

100 g (3½ oz) unsalted butter
1 tablespoon finely chopped fresh ginger
125 g (4½ oz/¾ cup) pine nuts, toasted (see method, page 215)
1 pinch chilli flakes
375 ml (13 fl oz/1½ cups) chicken stock
185 g (6½ oz/1 cup) couscous
155 g (5½ oz/1 cup) frozen peas, thawed
6 spring onions (scallions), thinly sliced with some green tops
1 handful coriander (cilantro) leaves, roughly chopped
finely grated zest of 2 limes
3 tablespoons lime juice
2 tablespoons extra virgin olive oil, plus extra, to serve
20 scallops, cleaned, roe on if possible
sea salt, to taste

Seared Scallops and Couscous.

The only time I saw scallops on my journey through Morocco was in Essaouira. We had them with a simple couscous salad. Scallops are one of my favourite ingredients and taste fantastic in this simple dish.

Melt the butter in a saucepan over medium heat. Add the ginger, pine nuts and chilli flakes. Cook for 3 minutes or until aromatic, then add the stock, increase the heat and bring to the boil.

Pour the hot stock mixture over the couscous in a bowl. Fold the peas into the couscous and cover the bowl with foil. Leave to steam for 5–10 minutes, or until the couscous is softened and cooked.

Fluff the grains with a fork and add the spring onion, coriander, lime zest and juice. Season well with sea salt and set aside.

Heat the oil in a frying pan over high heat. Season the scallops with sea salt and sear, in batches, for 20 seconds on each side, or until golden brown. Remove from the heat.

To serve, divide the couscous between four plates. Place the scallops on top, drizzle with a little extra virgin olive oil and add a sprinkle of sea salt.

SERVES 6

Laban Mutboukh
500 g (1 lb 2 oz/2 cups) plain yoghurt
1 egg white
2 teaspoons cornflour (cornstarch)

2 garlic cloves
2 teaspoons dried mint
60 g (2¼ oz/¼ cup) ghee or clarified butter
sea salt and ground white pepper, to taste
6 eggs

Laban Bil Bayd—Eggs in Yoghurt Garlic Sauce. An important part of this dish is the Laban Mutboukh, a cooked yoghurt base. Yoghurt is used in a lot of Middle Eastern cooking in much the same way Westerners use sour cream. It is important when making the Laban Mutboukh that you stir in the same direction all the time. This dish works well at breakfast or lunch.

To make the laban mutboukh, put the yoghurt in a heavy-based saucepan. Beat the egg white until frothy and add to the yoghurt with the cornflour and 1 teaspoon salt, making sure that you stir in the same direction until very well combined.

Place the pan over medium heat and stir constantly with a wooden spoon for 5 minutes, or until it begins to bubble. Simmer gently for 2–3 minutes until the mixture is thick and coats the back of a spoon. Remove from the heat, cover with a lid and keep warm. Preheat the oven to 200°C (400°F/Gas 6).

Pound the garlic cloves with the dried mint and ½ teaspoon salt in a mortar and pestle to make a coarse paste.

Heat the ghee in a small saucepan over low heat. Add the garlic and cook, stirring, for 2–3 minutes, or until aromatic.

Pour the warm laban mutboukh into an ovenproof dish with a 20 cm (8 in) diameter. Carefully break the eggs over the top, then pour over the garlic mix. Bake in the oven for about 15 minutes, or until the eggs are set. Season to taste and serve immediately.

SERVES 4

250 g (9 oz) clams (vongoles)
250 g (9 oz) mussels
100 ml (3½ fl oz) olive oil
1 large brown onion, roughly chopped
3 garlic cloves, thinly sliced
3 bay leaves
3 red capsicums (peppers), seeded and thinly sliced
½ teaspoon smoked paprika
500 g (1 lb 2 oz) tin diced tomatoes
170 ml (5½ fl oz/⅔ cup) white wine
2 pinches of saffron threads, infused in 250 ml (9 fl oz/1 cup) fish stock
175 g (6 oz) whole blanched almonds, toasted and roughly ground (see method, page 215)
sea salt and freshly ground black pepper, to taste
300 g (10½ oz) skinless, boneless firm white fish fillets, such as barramundi or sea bass, cut into chunks
300 g (10½ oz) skinless, boneless firm white fish fillets, such as blue-eye trevalla, cut into chunks

Fish Casserole with Almonds and Saffron. Around the harbour in Essaouira there were many stalls and restaurants where you could sit and eat the daily catch. One place served a terrific fish casserole. The dish was placed in the middle of the table and everyone helped themselves—I love this way of eating.

You can use a different fish in this if you have a favourite, but try to use two different varieties for a better result.

Soak the clams in cold water for 30 minutes. Scrub the mussels with a stiff brush and pull out the hairy beards. Discard any broken shellfish or ones that don't open when tapped on the bench. Rinse well and set aside.

In a large saucepan or deep flameproof casserole dish, heat the oil over medium heat. Add the onion, garlic and a pinch of salt and cook for 10 minutes, or until golden brown. Add the bay leaves and capsicum, reduce the heat and cook slowly over low heat for about 15 minutes, or until the capsicum is soft.

Add the paprika and tomatoes and cook for about 10 minutes, or until the tomato becomes pulpy. Add the wine and simmer for 5 minutes, or until reduced by half. Pour in the fish stock and saffron, simmer for about 10 minutes, then add the almonds. Season well, to taste. Finally, add the fish and shellfish. Stir into the sauce, then cover the pan or dish and simmer for about 8–10 minutes, or until the fish is opaque. Discard any unopened shellfish.

Serve with Moroccan Bread (see recipe, page 137) and Garlic and Saffron Mayonnaise (see recipe, page 214).

SERVES 6

200 ml (7 fl oz) olive oil
2 brown onions, thinly sliced
3 garlic cloves, thinly sliced
pinch of saffron threads, soaked in 3 tablespoons hot water
100 ml (3½ fl oz) white wine vinegar
300 ml (10½ fl oz) fish stock
2 tablespoons raisins
2 tablespoons pine nuts, lightly toasted (see method, page 215)
6 x 150 g (5½ oz) skinless, boneless firm white fish fillets, such as John Dory
20 baby vine tomatoes, cut in half
sea salt and freshly ground black pepper, to taste
coriander (cilantro) leaves, to garnish

Fish with Saffron, Pine Nuts and Raisins. If you can get it, use John Dory in this dish—it is such a beautiful fish to cook and eat. The simplicity of this dish is perfect.

Heat half the olive oil in a frying pan over medium heat and cook the onions and garlic for 8–10 minutes, or until lightly caramelized.

Add the saffron liquid and threads to the pan with the vinegar and fish stock and simmer for 2–3 minutes, then add the raisins and pine nuts. Remove from the heat. Set aside and keep warm.

Heat the remaining olive oil in a non-stick frying pan over medium heat. Fry the fish, for 2–3 minutes on one side, or until golden brown. Turn the fish and pour the onion mixture and tomatoes over the top. Continue to simmer for 2 minutes, or until the fish is opaque. Season, to taste.

Place a fish fillet on each plate and spoon the onion mixture and tomatoes over and around the fish. Garnish with the coriander and serve immediately.

THE WINDY CITY

Essaouira is steeped in history but also has a modern side with groups of tourists milling around souvenir stalls and enjoying the many good restaurants. There are some beautiful traditional riads within the old town, and for me these are the places to stay as they give you a real feel for the local hospitality and culture.

Seagulls can always be seen flying around the rampart walls of Essaouira, riding the powerful north-easterly trade winds as the waves crash over the rocks below. This wind is a part of the town's personality, flowing through the streets, and also attracts a crowd of eager windsurfers and kiteboarders.

SERVES 6

2 x 400 g (14 oz) whole barramundi (or sea bass or whiting), scaled, gutted and cleaned
200 ml (7 fl oz) olive oil
1 teaspoon turmeric
1 teaspoon cumin
1 teaspoon freshly ground black pepper
1 handful coriander (cilantro) leaves, finely chopped
800 g (1 lb 12 oz) tomatoes, roughly chopped
3 carrots, peeled and sliced
3 all-purpose potatoes, such as desiree, sliced
2 green capsicums (peppers), seeded and sliced
2 beef tomatoes, sliced
½ preserved lemon, pith removed, rinsed and zest finely sliced
20 green olives
sea salt and freshly ground black pepper, to taste

Fish Tagine. In Essaouira, we stayed at a beautiful little guesthouse overlooking the Atlantic Ocean. Fatima, who cooked our meals each day, made a wonderful fish tagine. We sat by the fire eating this delicious tagine with bread and wine, while the waves crashed over the rocks outside the window.

Cut each fish into three pieces (including the head). Set aside.

Put the olive oil, turmeric, cumin, pepper, coriander and chopped tomatoes in a large non-metallic bowl and stir to combine. Add the fish to the bowl and coat all over in the spice mixture.

Scatter the carrot slices in the bottom of a tagine or flameproof casserole dish with a lid. Lay the spiced fish pieces over the carrots. Add the potato slices to the spice mixture and coat well, then place a potato layer over the fish. Add a layer of capsicum and tomato slices. Pour any leftover spice mixture over the top of the sliced tomatoes and scatter the preserved lemon and olives evenly over the top. Season well and cover.

Cook over low heat for 45 minutes, or until the fish is opaque and cooked through to the bone. (Check after 20 minutes and add a little water if it looks dry—there should be just enough liquid to fill the bottom of the tagine.) Remove from the heat and serve with Moroccan Bread (see recipe, page 137).

Note: If your tagine is not used frequently you will need to season it before cooking (see method, page 216)

SERVES 4

Moroccan Potato Purée
500 g (1 lb 2 oz) all-purpose potatoes, such as desiree, peeled
3 garlic cloves, crushed
3 egg yolks
100 g (3½ oz) butter, diced
1 teaspoon ground cumin
2 teaspoons sweet paprika
½ teaspoon ground white pepper
2 tablespoons lemon juice
3 flat-leaf (Italian) parsley sprigs

100 ml (3½ fl oz) olive oil, plus extra, to serve
4 x 200 g (7 oz) swordfish steaks
sea salt and freshly ground black pepper, to taste

Pan-fried Swordfish with Moroccan Potato Purée. Seeing all the fish coming in daily to Essaouira was an awesome sight. There is something about being at the docks when the catch comes in, with the seagulls screeching overhead, waiting for a bite themselves. This potato dish is superb—don't rush it, fold the ingredients in carefully—and the flavour of the fresh swordfish completes it wonderfully.

To make the Moroccan potato purée, boil the potatoes in a saucepan of salted water for 15 minutes, or until easily pierced with a sharp knife. Drain and leave to stand for 5 minutes to dry out. Mash to a smooth purée.

Fold the garlic, egg yolks and butter through the puréed potato and mix well. Add the cumin, paprika, white pepper, lemon juice and ½ teaspoon salt and mix thoroughly. Cover and keep warm.

Heat the olive oil in a frying pan over high heat. Season the swordfish steaks with salt and pepper and cook for 2–3 minutes, or until browned. Turn over and cook for 1 minute further or until the fish is opaque. Remove the steaks from the pan and drain on paper towel.

Just before serving, fold the parsley through the potato purée. Divide the purée between serving bowls and place a swordfish steak over the mash. Drizzle a little olive oil over the top and serve immediately.

SERVES 6

100 ml (3½ fl oz) olive oil
2 farmed rabbits, cleaned, washed and cut into pieces (ask your butcher to do this for you)
1 teaspoon ras el hanout (see recipe, page 215)
1 teaspoon rosewater
¼ teaspoon freshly grated nutmeg
½ teaspoon freshly grated ginger
½ teaspoon ground white pepper
½ teaspoon ground cumin
3 brown onions, thinly sliced
8 garlic cloves, crushed
1 large handful flat-leaf (Italian) parsley sprigs
1 large handful coriander (cilantro) sprigs
1.5 litres (52 fl oz/6 cups) chicken stock
salt and freshly ground black pepper, to taste

Spiced Rabbit. I didn't know Moroccans loved rabbit until I saw the rabbits sitting in cages next to the chickens in the marketplace in Essaouira, awaiting their fate. You can substitute hare or partridge in this recipe, although with its delicate flavour and the tenderness of the meat, rabbit is perfect for this dish.

Heat half the oil in a large frying pan over medium heat and cook the rabbit for 6–8 minutes, to seal on all sides until golden brown. Remove from the pan and set aside.

Add the remaining oil to the pan, then the ras el hanout, rosewater, nutmeg, ginger, pepper, cumin and ½ teaspoon salt. Lightly fry the spices for about 2 minutes, stirring constantly, or until aromatic. Add the onions and garlic and cook for 8–10 minutes, or until lightly browned.

Return the rabbit to the pan and stir to coat with the spices and onions. Add the parsley, coriander and stock and bring to the boil. Reduce the heat and simmer for 40 minutes, or until the rabbit is tender. Remove the rabbit from the pan and keep warm.

Increase the heat and return the liquid to the boil and cook for 15–20 minutes, or until the sauce has thickened slightly. Season, to taste. Remove from the heat and pour the sauce over the rabbit in a large serving dish. This dish tastes great served with buttered mashed potatoes.

The Berbers of Morocco

When merchants and traders came to Morocco from far-off kingdoms, they brought with them the treasures of many different civilizations—exotic foods, art, music and religion. They came to trade with the various tribes of a people known collectively as the Berbers, who prize family and religion above all else and still live as they have done for many, many generations. The Berbers are survivors; they perform miracles with the little they have. Their greatest asset has been their strong sense of family and community. Life on the land is tough; as a result the community works together and looks after each other. This has ensured Berber culture has not only survived but thrived into the twenty-first century.

There is no better place to see this than a traditional Berber farm. I visited the Marit family from Doowah, Arganga, just down the coast from Essaouira. Over the past four centuries, five generations of this family have lived and worked the land here. As the family grew, so did the farm—all the animals are housed inside the walls every night and the farm is now a complex of grand proportions.

Generally speaking, fifty or so houses make up a Berber village of a few extended families. Fifty to a hundred villages make up a tribe. It's a culture with a strict gender divide: Berber women run things around the home and men are responsible for the manual work in the fields.

Once fearsome pirates and renowned warrior horsemen, the Berbers are now expert farmers with an ability to raise crops and livestock in what I would describe as harsh desert.

Water is obviously the most precious commodity. Farms have to rely on the unreliable seasonal rains. Miraculously, even with so little rainfall and a rocky terrain that resembles a Martian landscape, these farmers manage to do the impossible. Several times I saw farm workers ploughing what looked like fields of boulders and thought how futile it was, only to see similar plots up the road lush with healthy green crops. The rocks are used for building houses, and solid walls that mark out land boundaries.

With all the difficulties of desert farming, the Marits manage to be largely self-sufficient. They grow wheat and vegetables and tend livestock, and this provides them with the ingredients to make one of the essentials of Berber cooking—couscous. (You haven't lived until you've tried Mrs Marit's couscous.)

Unlike life in the cities, where lunch is a two- or three-hour affair, in the country breakfast is the traditional time for the family to get together and talk before the working day begins.

Wherever you go in the world, bread is usually the staff of life and in Morocco it is no different. Here bread is made from wheat or barley, comes flat and still warm from the

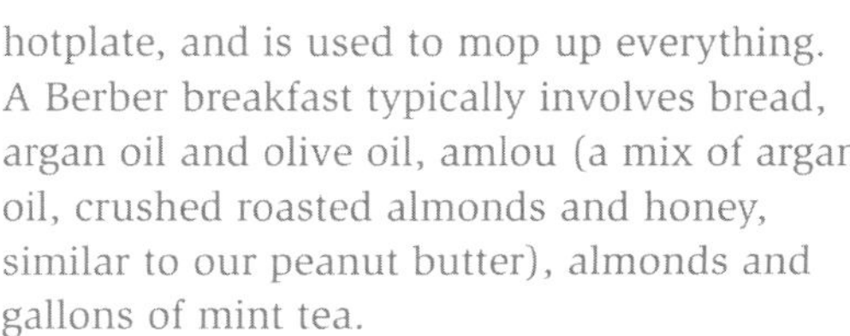

hotplate, and is used to mop up everything. A Berber breakfast typically involves bread, argan oil and olive oil, amlou (a mix of argan oil, crushed roasted almonds and honey, similar to our peanut butter), almonds and gallons of mint tea.

Tree-climbing goats are a curious feature in this part of Morocco, and there is only one tree they climb: the argan tree. This tree only grows in a small area in the south-west of Morocco, between Essaouira and Agadir. Its oil and by-products have been used locally over the centuries for many things, but it's only recently that the rest of the world has become aware of the amazing properties of this unique tree. In 1999, UNESCO recognized the importance of the argan tree by placing it on the World Heritage List. This was some time before argan oil was loudly proclaimed as a potential therapeutic gold mine.

There are roughly 21 million argan trees growing in the area and they play a vital role in the food chain and the environment. The fruit is green and fleshy, like an olive, but larger and rounder. Inside, there is a nut with an extremely hard shell. It contains up to three almond-shaped kernels.

Pharmaceutical companies, non-government organizations and the European Union are all funding research projects into argan's medicinal uses. Prime among its health-promoting properties are its abilities to lower bad cholesterol and increase good cholesterol levels, stimulate circulation and strengthen the body's immune system. This means it could be very useful in treating some big health problems, including cardiovascular and rheumatic diseases, and HIV/AIDS. Argan is also a miracle oil for both greying parents and their teenage children—not only does it beautify the skin, but it also makes a brilliant hair conditioner and nail strengthener, and it seems to cure juvenile acne.

Argan production is still basically a cottage industry managed largely by women. In the village of Tanana, a women's co-operative has been set up for argan production. It aims to improve and certify the quality of argan oil, preserve the environment by replanting argan trees, ensure satisfactory working conditions and encourage sustainable development.

Traditionally, goats ate the fruit, and the hard nut was excreted intact. Later, the nuts would be collected by farmers to produce the oil. The production of argan oil still employs traditional methods, and it's a lengthy process. Soumya, the proud manager of the women's co-operative, explained to me the steps involved in extracting the miracle oil.

The first step is to peel the fruit and to find the nut inside. It looks like a large olive pip. The skins are fed to animals because they are very high in nutrients. The second step is to break the nuts open to get to the argan kernels inside. The shells are used to fuel fires. Argan kernels are very bitter, so they are roasted in a large pan over a fire to reduce the bitterness. Then the kernels are crushed in a mortar and pestle to extract the liquid—it looks like something between an oil and a paste. The women knead it by hand and slowly add warm water to separate the oil from the paste.

It will take one woman six days to produce one litre of argan oil from 60 kilograms (132 pounds) of fruit. Households that press their own argan oil tend to use it in their food preparation. It is usually used as a dressing, as heat destroys the beneficial qualities. It is used for flavouring salads, and also a few drops can be stirred into couscous just before serving to give it a rich, nutty aroma.

As well as argan oil, the inhabitants of Amagor, a village in the foothills of the Small Atlas Mountains, have been making olive oil in the traditional way for centuries. Olives have become very important to the economy, and Morocco is now the world's second largest exporter, after Greece. Many farmers and village co-operatives make their own oil. The participants are all paid in oil, with the owner of the mill getting two litres, the workers two litres, and even the mule being paid its share!

The olives are pressed in a traditional 'maasra' or pressing plant—they say this brings out the best flavour. The olives are first ground using a huge grinding stone that takes four months to sculpt from solid rock. The crushed olive mash is shovelled into large, flat wicker baskets called *sourdins*, and loaded into a giant press. The partially filtered oil flows away into a pit. The whole procedure is then repeated for a second pressing, then water is added and the pure oil is simply scooped off the top. The result is nothing short of divine.

Nothing is wasted: after the olive mash is pressed, the dried pulp that remains is used for the fire. At seven in the morning, the aroma in the mill is truly memorable.

MAKES 20 PORTIONS

zest of ½ orange (peeled into strips, white pith removed)
1 small rosemary sprig
2 thyme sprigs
1 oregano sprig
1 fresh bay leaf, cut into four
60 ml (2 fl oz/¼ cup) extra virgin olive oil
½ preserved lemon, rinsed well
1 long red chilli, thinly sliced (julienne)
6 garlic cloves, peeled
500 g (1 lb 2 oz/2¾ cups) mixed olives

Marinated Olives. It's easy to buy ready-made marinated olives, but why not try making your own? Once you have all the ingredients, it's quick and simple. Then you just need to warm them slightly before eating them.

Lay the orange zest on a chopping board and bang the shiny side with the back of a large knife to release the oils. Roll the herbs with your hands to release the oils and flavour from them.

Put the olive oil, herbs, orange zest, preserved lemon, chilli and garlic into a non-metallic bowl.

Steep the olives in boiling water for 1 minute only. Drain the olives well, place them in the bowl and toss them in the marinade.

Cover the bowl with plastic wrap and allow to marinate for 3 hours. Then place the olives and marinade in a sterilized airtight container (see method, page 216). Olives will keep for a few days, stored in the refrigerator.

SERVES 4–6

250 g (9 oz/2 cups) green pitted olives, coarsely chopped
60 ml (2 fl oz/¼ cup) olive oil
400 g (14 oz) tin chopped tomatoes
2 garlic cloves, crushed
½ red onion, finely chopped
2 teaspoons tomato passata (puréed tomatoes)
½ teaspoon paprika
¼ teaspoon cayenne pepper

Olive Dip.

With an abundance of olive groves in Morocco you can't help but love them—there are many varieties, sizes and textures and they are available in every souk, presented in every way possible. Olives are like good wine, the flavour needs to be carefully nurtured out of the fruit. This is a great dip to serve with drinks as a light snack.

Steep the olives in boiling water for 1 minute. Drain well and set aside.

Heat the olive oil in a saucepan over medium heat. Add the tomato, garlic, onion and tomato passata and bring to the boil. Reduce the heat and simmer for 5 minutes, then add the paprika, cayenne pepper, olives and 60 ml (2 fl oz/ ¼ cup) water. Simmer gently for about 15 minutes, or until thick. Remove from the heat and allow to cool to room temperature before refrigerating overnight. Serve chilled with Moroccan Bread (see recipe, opposite).

MAKES 8 ROLLS

3 teaspoons dry yeast
2 teaspoons caster (superfine) sugar
500 g (1 lb 2 oz/4 cups) fine semolina, plus extra, for dusting

Moroccan Bread. Bread is a staple in Morocco; it is eaten with every meal and is plentiful on the table. There is something special about making fresh bread—the smell of it baking in the kitchen is nothing short of divine—not to mention eating the finished result!

Dissolve the yeast and sugar in 1½ tablespoons warm water and leave until it starts to bubble.

Mix the semolina and 2 teaspoons salt on a bench. Make a well in the middle and pour in the yeast mixture, along with 310 ml (10¾ fl oz/ 1¼ cups) warm water.

Using your fingertips, start to work in all the semolina, starting from outside the well and working inwards as you go. Only add enough water to make a firm dough. (The amount of water will vary depending on the type of semolina you're using and even the weather on the day you are baking.) Knead the dough for about 10 minutes, or until the dough is smooth and elastic.

Divide into 8 even-sized balls. Dust to coat each ball with semolina, and cover with a dry tea towel (dish towel). Set aside in a warm place to rise for 1½–2 hours, or until doubled in size.

Preheat the oven to 200°C (400°F/Gas 6). Grease a large baking tray.

Flatten the dough balls into discs about 2 cm (¾ in) thick. Prick them with a fork a few times and place on the baking tray. Bake for 10–20 minutes, or until golden brown and cooked through. For the best flavour, serve while still warm.

SERVES 4

6 roma (plum) tomatoes, seeded and diced
1 telegraph (long) cucumber, seeded and diced
1 red onion, finely diced
1 green capsicum (pepper), seeded and finely diced
1 handful chopped flat-leaf (Italian) parsley
1 teaspoon cumin seeds, dry-roasted and ground (see method, page 216)
4 tablespoons lemon juice
100 ml (3½ fl oz) olive oil
sea salt and freshly ground black pepper, to taste

Moroccan Tomato and Cucumber Salad.

I'm a great fan of salads at any time of the year and this recipe is simplicity itself. It can be used as a starter, or to accompany grilled fish or meat.

Place the tomato, cucumber, onion and capsicum in a large non-metallic mixing bowl.

In a smaller bowl, combine the parsley, cumin, lemon juice and olive oil and stir thoroughly. Pour the dressing over the vegetables and toss thoroughly to coat. Season, to taste.

SERVES 4

60 ml (2 fl oz/¼ cup) olive oil
2 red capsicums (peppers), grilled, peeled and diced (see method, page 215)
2 green capsicums (peppers), grilled, peeled and diced (see method, page 215)
2 yellow capsicums (peppers), grilled, peeled and diced (see method, page 215)
3 flat-leaf (Italian) parsley sprigs, finely chopped
3 coriander (cilantro) sprigs, finely chopped
3 garlic cloves, crushed
1 tablespoon sweet paprika
½ teaspoon hot chilli powder
½ teaspoon ground cumin

Tchoutchouka Salad. This salad is actually Algerian but I tasted it first in Morocco, served with grilled fish. You'll experience an amazing burst of flavours when you eat this—the sweet flavours of the roast capsicums offsets the spices and herbs perfectly.

Heat the oil in a large frying pan over low–medium heat. Add the capsicums, parsley, coriander, garlic, paprika, chilli, cumin and ¼ teaspoon salt. Cook gently for about 30 minutes, stirring constantly, or until all the juices are absorbed. Remove from the heat. This salad can be served hot or cold.

SERVES 8

170 ml (5½ fl oz/⅔ cup) vegetable oil
4 brown onions, sliced
1 teaspoon sherry vinegar
200 g (7 oz) soft goat's cheese
85 g (3 oz) mascarpone cheese
2 egg yolks
½ teaspoon ground allspice
500 g (1 lb 2 oz) filo pastry
25 g (1 oz) butter, melted
150 g (5½ oz) English spinach, blanched and drained well

Goat's Cheese Tartlets. Only in Morocco can you see goats hanging out in trees as you drive along the roads. The goats climb to reach the fruit of the argan tree, which they love.

There is also plenty of goat's cheese in Morocco. This tart really highlights the flavour of the cheese.

Heat the oil in a saucepan over low heat. Add the onions and cook slowly, stirring occasionally, for about 45 minutes, or until they are a deep golden brown and very soft. Drain off the excess oil and stir through the sherry vinegar and ½ teaspoon salt. Set aside.

To make the filling, mix together the goat's cheese, mascarpone, egg yolks and allspice in a mixing bowl.

Preheat the oven to 200°C (400°F/Gas 6). Lightly grease 8 loose-based tart tins with a 10 cm (4 in) diameter.

Cut the pastry into 14 cm (5½ in) squares and line the base and side of each tartlet tin with 5 sheets of pastry, buttering each sheet and placing them one on top of the other as you go, so that the pastry overhangs the tins. Put the tins in the refrigerator for about 30 minutes to rest.

Bake in the oven for 15 minutes, or until golden brown. Remove from the oven and allow to cool.

Divide the onion between the pastry cases, then divide the spinach evenly over the onion and fill to the top with the cheese mixture. Bake the tarts for 10–15 minutes, or until the top is golden and puffed and the centre is creamy. Remove the tarts from the tins and serve with a green salad.

SERVES 4

750 g (1 lb 10 oz) minced (ground) lamb
5 garlic cloves, crushed
½ teaspoon ground allspice
1 teaspoon ground coriander
1 teaspoon paprika
1 large handful chopped coriander (cilantro) leaves
100 ml (3½ fl oz) olive oil, plus extra for pan-frying
1 brown onion, finely chopped
400 g (14 oz) tin chopped tomatoes
1 tablespoon tomato paste (concentrated purée)
1 tablespoon honey
salt and freshly ground black pepper, to taste
4 eggs

Kefta Meatballs with Tomato and Egg. This recipe is a great way to start making tagines, as it's so simple and quick to make. It's also very tasty.

In a mixing bowl, mix the lamb, 3 cloves of garlic, spices and half the chopped coriander until it is all thoroughly combined. With wet hands, roll the mixture into 24 walnut-sized balls and set aside.

Heat the oil in a saucepan over low heat. Add the onion and the remaining garlic and cook for 5 minutes, or until they are soft but not coloured. Add the tomatoes, tomato paste and honey and cook for about 10 minutes, or until the sauce thickens slightly. Season to taste. Remove from the heat and set aside until needed.

Heat the extra oil in a frying pan over medium heat and cook the meatballs, in two batches, for 6–8 minutes each, or until golden brown.

Transfer the meatballs to a tagine or flameproof casserole dish with a lid and pour the tomato sauce over the meatballs. Place over medium heat and bring just to the boil, then reduce the heat, cover with a lid and simmer for 15–20 minutes, or until the meatballs are tender and the sauce has thickened slightly. Stir occasionally to prevent the sauce sticking to the bottom of the tagine. Break the eggs over the top of the meatballs and continue to cook for 10 minutes, or until the eggs are just set. Season to taste, sprinkle with the remaining chopped coriander and serve immediately.

Note: If your tagine is not used frequently you will need to season it before cooking (see method, page 216).

SERVES 4

100 ml (3½ fl oz) olive oil, plus extra, to serve
1 red onion, finely chopped
1 teaspoon ground turmeric
1 teaspoon ground coriander
1 teaspoon paprika
10 tomatoes, peeled (see method, page 215) and diced
1 handful chopped coriander (cilantro) leaves
7 eggs, beaten
salt and freshly ground black pepper, to taste

Berber Tagine Omelette. This recipe was a great find. We were travelling across the High Atlas Mountains and stopped for lunch. We were told that we would be served omelette with bread and salad, and this is what came out. It was so good, I brought the recipe back to my restaurant, where it is now a permanent fixture on the breakfast menu.

Preheat the oven to 180°C (350°F/Gas 4).

Heat a tagine or a flameproof casserole dish with a lid over medium heat. Add the olive oil and onion and cook slowly for about 5 minutes, stirring often, or until soft. Add the spices and cook for 2 minutes to release the flavours.

Add the tomatoes and coriander, then reduce the heat and simmer, stirring often, for about 10–15 minutes, or until the sauce thickens. Remove from the heat and pour the beaten eggs over the sauce.

Cover with a lid and place in the oven for about 10–15 minutes, or until the omelette is lightly puffed and the egg sets. Season well and drizzle with a little extra olive oil. Serve with slices of crusty bread.

Note: If your tagine is not used frequently you will need to season it before cooking (see method, page 216)

SERVES 6

8 dried dates, cut in half
8 dried apricots, cut in half
8 dried prunes, cut in half
8 dried figs, cut in half
60 g (2¼ oz) unsalted butter
45 g (1½ oz/¼ cup) soft brown sugar
100 ml (3½ fl oz) sweet wine
¼ teaspoon ground cinnamon
1 cinnamon stick, broken in half
½ pineapple, peeled, cored and cut into 2 cm (¾ in) dice
2 corella pears, cored and then each cut into 8 wedges
clotted cream, to serve

Cinnamon Poached Fruits. Marrakech is at the perfect altitude for growing dates. There were many stalls in the souks selling a variety of dates, dried fruits and nuts. This dessert is perfect for cold winter nights. You can use different fruits if you wish, or add other winter fruits.

Put the dried fruit in a bowl and cover with warm water. Leave to rest for 4 hours, then drain well.

Melt the butter in a saucepan over medium heat and add the sugar, sweet wine, ground cinnamon and the cinnamon stick and bring to the boil. Add the soaked dried fruits and cook for about 5 minutes, stirring constantly, or until the fruit starts to soften. Add the pineapple and pear, reduce the heat and simmer for about 10 minutes, or until the pears are tender. Stir gently, being careful not to break up the fruits when mixing.

Divide the fruit evenly between individual bowls and pour the syrup over the top. Serve with clotted cream.

COUSCOUS

Couscous is one of the essentials of Berber cooking. The traditional way of making couscous involves semolina, water, flour, and a lot of sieving. Then it's hands on to separate the hot steaming grains. The grains are left overnight to dry, and the next day there's even more finger-work, this time with oil. Of course, today in the Western world we don't have to make it from scratch and can simply buy it in a packet from the supermarket. It is as simple as adding boiling water to cook the grains. The difference, however, is in the taste.

Imperial Fez

The Holy City of Fez has been described poetically as an immense piece of jewellery studded with emeralds, pearls and amethysts.

There are more than 300 mosques dotted throughout the 260 hectares (642 acres) of the medina. It is said that Fez is a mystery that reveals itself little by little. It's one of the finest medieval cities in the world, and UNESCO has declared it a World Heritage site.

Over a thousand years ago, as Europe slumbered through the Dark Ages, Fez was a thriving trading, religious and intellectual centre and to this day it is considered the academic capital of the country. So why was this city such a magnet for cultural, intellectual and religious life? The answer, of course, was trade. As trade opened up along the caravan routes, Fez was in a perfect geographical position. Exotic foods, ideas and goods arrived along with a new religion—Islam—and, in the process, Fez grew fabulously wealthy, both commercially and spiritually. This meant more people were able to consider pursuits beyond mere survival. So, in the year 859 AD the great Karaouiyne University was established, making it now the oldest university in the world. Fez quickly became an educational centre for the entire region, its influence spreading far beyond the kingdom's boundaries.

These days the old imperial city is a warren of countless streets, with no visible means of identifying them. No vehicles are allowed inside the old medina, and there are even one-way streets for the only form of transport, the mule or donkey. These four-legged couriers do have some connection with the car, though—their hooves are shod with pieces of old rubber tyres. This muffles the sound and makes it safer negotiating the narrow cobbled lanes.

Fez's markets hold stalls with amazing produce you simply can't get anywhere else. Naturally, the usual varieties of fruit and vegetables, herbs and spices are there in abundance. Camel is a delicacy, mainly eaten in the south, and I'm told that it is a lot leaner and lower in fat than beef. All parts of the animal are used—even the camel hump is minced with the meat. All meat in Morocco is halal, which means the animal is slaughtered in a certain way. The butcher needs to be a devout Muslim who prays five times a day. Pointing the animal towards Mecca, he utters the word '*Bismillah*', which means 'in the name of Allah', and swiftly proceeds to sever the windpipe and arteries in the neck. This ensures a quick, painless death.

It's said that although you can find great examples of craftsmanship all over

Morocco, you'll find the best-quality pieces originated in Fez. The old city is full of ancient workshops, making everything from traditional handmade clothing like *jellabas* to ceramics, metal items and leather goods. You can't come to Fez without visiting the famous medieval tannery; it's like a scene from a mythical underworld. Tanning is hard, smelly work because the only way to make sure each skin is properly treated is to tread in the pungent liquid—a mixture of dye and pigeon poo, which softens the leather and is a natural fixative. You'll see skins laid out drying in the sun on the slopes of the surrounding hillsides, as well as covering every rooftop in the tannery.

These days, tourists flock from all points of the compass and, with its expanding population, the ancient city is bursting at the seams. As in Venice, many of the old buildings are suffering and need loving attention. After declaring Fez a World Heritage site, UNESCO began one of the largest restoration projects in the world. It's expected to cost US$600 million, and will take 20 years to complete.

Throughout the month of Ramadan, when Muslims fast during daylight hours, the first dish served after sunset is a hearty, spicy dish called harira. Harira is virtually the national soup of Morocco, and during Ramadan you can smell its spicy aroma wafting through the streets at sunset. It's a rich vegetable and lentil broth, prescribed in the Koran as the perfect meal for the faithful. There are many variations of the recipe, with meat or chicken often being added (see recipe, page 156). Harira is usually accompanied by dates and sticky honey cakes, but I like it best with crusty chunks of freshly baked bread.

I loved exploring the colour of the souks, the flavours of the food, and meeting the proud, gentle people of the Holy City of Fez.

SERVES 4

Marinade
100 g (3½ oz) Greek-style yoghurt
2 teaspoons harissa (see recipe, pages 214–15)
2 teaspoons ground cumin
2 teaspoons ground coriander
2 garlic cloves, crushed
1 tablespoon olive oil
salt and freshly ground black pepper, to taste
4 chicken breasts, skinned
375 ml (13 fl oz/1½ cups) chicken stock
1 teaspoon ground cinnamon
250 g (9 oz/1⅓ cups) couscous
400 g (14 oz) tin chickpeas, rinsed and drained
2 red capsicums (peppers), roasted, skinned, seeded and sliced (see method, page 215)
100 g (3½ oz/⅔ cup) sun-dried tomatoes
3 tablespoons lime juice
1 small handful mint, chopped
1 small handful coriander (cilantro) sprigs, chopped, plus extra, to garnish

Moroccan Chicken Salad. One of the wonderful things about travelling through the Middle East was that I came to a deeper understanding of the use of spices. Spices can make such a difference to a dish, but if not used properly they can overpower it. This is a great salad, something a little different from the norm, which is sure to impress.

To make the marinade, mix the yoghurt, harissa, cumin, coriander, garlic and olive oil in a bowl. Season, to taste, then spread the marinade over the chicken breasts. Place the chicken breasts in a non-metallic dish, cover and refrigerate for 2–3 hours, to allow the flavours to develop.

Preheat the oven to 200°C (400°F/Gas 6). Put the chicken in a small roasting tin and cook for 20–25 minutes, or until tender. Press the thickest part of the breast to test—it should be firm to touch. Remove from the oven, cover with foil, and rest in a warm place for 10 minutes.

Meanwhile, put the chicken stock and cinnamon in a saucepan over high heat. Bring to the boil, then add the couscous and stir to combine. Remove from the heat, cover and leave to rest for 5–10 minutes.

Transfer the couscous to a large bowl, fluff with a fork to separate the grains, then add the chickpeas, capsicum, sun-dried tomatoes, lime juice, mint and coriander.

Slice each chicken breast into six or eight pieces. Gently mix into the salad. Garnish with the extra coriander leaves and serve immediately.

SERVES 4–6

500 g (1 lb 2 oz) carrots, peeled and sliced into 5 mm (¼ in) rounds
60 ml (2 fl oz/¼ cup) white wine vinegar
1 teaspoon ground cumin
1 teaspoon paprika
1½ teaspoons caster (superfine) sugar
2 tablespoons lemon juice
1 handful coriander (cilantro) leaves, roughly chopped
sea salt, to taste

Restaurant Zora's Carrot Salad. You would never find Restaurant Zora without the help of a local, and even the one who showed us the way found it difficult. To be honest, I had never been a fan of boiled carrots until I ate them at Restaurant Zora. Like many good dishes, they are simple to make.

Cook the carrots in a large saucepan of boiling salted water until just tender. Drain and refresh in cold water, then drain again.

In a bowl, mix together the vinegar, cumin, paprika and sugar. Stir in the carrots, making sure they are well coated with the spice mix. Finish by mixing in the lemon juice and coriander. Season with sea salt, to taste and serve as an appetizer with dips and breads.

SERVES 6

100 g (3½ oz) coriander chutney (see recipe, page 25)
1 teaspoon ground cumin
1 teaspoon ground turmeric
1 teaspoon paprika
½ preserved lemon, pith removed, rinsed and chopped
100 ml (3½ fl oz) vegetable oil
1 litre (35 fl oz/4 cups) chicken stock, plus 100 ml (3½ fl oz) extra
2 kg (4 lb 8 oz) whole chicken
5 red onions, finely diced
1 large handful coriander (cilantro) leaves, chopped
120 g (4¼ oz) soft butter

Fez Chicken.

This is an interesting recipe as the chicken is first poached, then roasted to finish it. Stunning aromas are produced while cooking—and it is even better to eat.

Mix the coriander chutney, cumin, turmeric, paprika, ½ teaspoon salt and half of the preserved lemon in a bowl. Add the oil and 100 ml (3½ fl oz) of the stock, stirring well to combine.

Carefully loosen the skin over the chicken breasts by inserting your fingers between the skin and breast meat. Using clean hands, rub half the mix all over the chicken, inside and out, and under the breast skin, being careful not to tear it. Place the chicken in a large stockpot or saucepan with a lid.

Add the onions, remaining spice mix, coriander, remaining preserved lemon and chicken stock to the pot. Cover the pot and bring to the boil over high heat. Reduce the heat and simmer for 1½ hours. Preheat the oven to 180°C (350°F/Gas 4).

Remove the chicken from the pot—tipping any excess fluid from the cavity back into the pot—and place on a roasting tray. Put the butter on top of the chicken and roast in the oven for 20–30 minutes, or until golden brown. Leave to rest for 10 minutes before carving.

To serve, cut the chicken into pieces and divide between individual plates with a spoonful of the cooking liquor and some onion and lemon. This is great served with Moroccan Bread (see recipe, page 137) and Moroccan Tomato and Cucumber Salad (see recipe, page 138).

SERVES 6

pinch of saffron threads
150 ml (5 fl oz) olive oil
4 chicken breasts, cut into 1.5 cm (5/8 in) dice
2 garlic cloves, crushed
3 celery sticks, finely diced
1 carrot, finely diced
1 brown onion, finely diced
3 tablespoons grated fresh ginger
800 g (1 lb 12 oz) tin tomatoes
1 teaspoon ground cumin
100 g (3½ oz/½ cup) small blue-green (Puy-style) lentils
100 g (3½ oz) tin chickpeas, rinsed and drained
1 litre (35 fl oz/4 cups) chicken stock
100 g (3½ oz/½ cup) long-grain rice
2½ tablespoons lemon juice
sea salt and freshly ground black pepper, to taste
1 handful coriander (cilantro) leaves, chopped
harissa (see recipe, pages 214–15), to serve (optional)

Harira Soup with Chicken. Harira soup is traditionally served during the month of Ramadan to break the fast. It can be used as a first course or, with the chicken added, as a meal in itself.

Infuse the saffron in 3 tablespoons boiling water for about 2–3 minutes.

In a large saucepan, heat half the oil over medium–high heat and cook the diced chicken, in batches, for 5 minutes, turning to seal on all sides. Remove the chicken from the pan and set aside. Refrigerate until needed.

In the same pan, heat the remaining oil. Add the garlic, celery, carrot and onion, and cook, stirring often, for 6–8 minutes, or until the onion is soft. Add the ginger, tomato, saffron water, cumin, lentils, chickpeas and chicken stock. Bring to the boil, then reduce the heat and simmer for about 20 minutes. Add the rice and chicken and simmer for a further 15 minutes, or until the rice is tender.

Season with the lemon juice, salt and pepper, to taste. Just before serving, add the coriander. If you prefer a spicier soup, season with some harissa. This soup tastes great served with Moroccan Bread (see recipe, page 137).

SERVES 6

100 g (3½ oz) unsalted butter
2 tablespoons caster (superfine) sugar
500 g (1 lb 2 oz/2¾ cups) couscous, cooked (see method, page 214)
100 g (3½ oz/⅔ cup) pistachio nuts
100 g (3½ oz/¾ cup) sultanas (golden raisins)
100 g (3½ oz/⅔ cup) almonds, toasted (see method, page 215)
100 g (3½ oz/¾ cup) raisins
icing (confectioner's) sugar, to serve
ground cinnamon, to serve
pomegranate molasses, to serve (see glossary)

Sweet Couscous. We don't usually think of couscous as a sweet dish, but this is a fantastic dessert option. The sweetness works so well with the texture of the couscous, fruits and nuts. Make sure you add the pomegranate molasses at the end.

Add the butter and sugar to the warm couscous and stir to combine, fluffing the hot grains with a fork.

Add the pistachios, sultanas, almonds and raisins and stir to combine. Serve the sweet couscous on a large platter and dust with icing sugar and cinnamon. To finish, drizzle the pomegranate molasses over the top.

MAKES 40 PIECES

300 g (10½ oz/3 cups) ground almonds
150 g (5½ oz/1¼ cups) icing (confectioner's) sugar, plus extra, for dusting
1 teaspoon ground cinnamon
2 eggs, beaten
finely grated zest of 1 lemon
60 ml (2 fl oz/¼ cup) orange blossom water
450 g (1 lb/3⅔ cups) plain (all-purpose) flour
2 tablespoons unsalted butter, melted

Gazelles' Horns. These are crescent-shaped little pastries that are often served with mint tea after a meal. I had fun making these while in Fez, but they are even more fun to eat!

Put the ground almonds in a mixing bowl and sift in the icing sugar and cinnamon. Add the eggs, lemon zest and 1 tablespoon of orange blossom water and stir to combine. Cover with plastic wrap and refrigerate until needed.

Sift the flour into a mixing bowl, make a well in the centre and add the melted butter and a pinch of salt. Using clean hands, work the mixture into a smooth elastic dough, adding the remaining orange blossom water in small amounts until it is all combined.

Preheat the oven to 180°C (350°F/Gas 4). Lightly grease a baking tray, the bench and a rolling pin with butter. Divide the dough into two equal portions. Roll each one out until it is a 30 x 30 cm (12 x 12 in) square and 3 mm (⅛ in) thick.

Remove the almond filling from the refrigerator and place teaspoons of the filling at 3 cm (1¼ in) intervals along one edge of pastry.

Lift the same edge and carefully stretch it outwards, folding it over the mounds of almond filling to just cover the mixture.

Using a biscuit cutter, cut around each almond mound, making the almond its centre. Pinch the outside edges together into a crescent shape, similar to a gazelle's horn. Prick each one with a fork a couple of times. Repeat this process until all the pastry and almond mixture is used—you should make about 40 in total.

Place the horns on the prepared tray and bake for about 15 minutes, or until dry to the touch (the pastries should not colour).

Remove from the oven and dust with icing sugar. Allow to cool and serve.

SERVES 6

500 ml (17 fl oz/2 cups) full-cream (whole) milk
1 vanilla bean, split lengthways
4 egg yolks
2 whole eggs
250 g (9 oz/1 cup) caster (superfine) sugar

Dates
55 g (2 oz/¼ cup) caster (superfine) sugar
3 tablespoons rosewater
12 fresh dates, cut in half, stones removed

Crème Caramel with Dates and Rosewater.

When travelling, you see how much the French have influenced the world of cuisine. One of the dishes you'll see everywhere is the classic crème caramel. It is a simple dessert that is recognized globally. Here it was served with a Moroccan twist—dates cooked in a sugar syrup with rosewater.

Place the milk and vanilla bean in a saucepan over medium heat. Bring to the boil, then remove from the heat and allow to rest for 15 minutes to allow the flavours to infuse.

Put the egg yolks, whole eggs and 115 g (4 oz/½ cup) sugar in a separate bowl and whisk together until well combined.

Remove the vanilla bean from the warm milk and then whisk the milk into the eggs. Strain through a fine sieve and allow to cool.

To make the caramel, put the remaining sugar and 80 ml (2½ fl oz/⅓ cup) water in a saucepan over medium–high heat. Stir to dissolve the sugar, then bring to the boil and cook for 10 minutes, or until caramelized. Remove from the heat and put the saucepan immediately into a sink filled with cold water to stop the cooking process. (Be careful not to get any water into the caramel.) Divide the caramel between 6 lightly greased 125 ml (4 fl oz/½ cup) ramekins or dariole moulds. Preheat the oven to 100°C (200°F/Gas ½).

After about 5 minutes, or when the caramel has set, pour the custard mixture into the ramekins, almost to the top. Place the moulds in a baking tray and pour enough water into the tray to come halfway up the sides of the ramekins. Cover the tray with foil and cook for 40 minutes, or until set. To test, tap the side of the ramekin—there should be a slight wobble. Once set, remove from the oven, take the ramekins out of the tray, cool slightly and place in the refrigerator to chill.

To prepare the dates, bring the sugar, rosewater and 200 ml (7 fl oz) water to the boil and stir until the sugar has dissolved. Reduce the heat, add the dates and simmer for about 15 minutes, or until they have softened.

To serve, run a knife around the edge of the crème caramels to release them and invert onto serving plates. Spoon the dates alongside and drizzle with rosewater syrup.

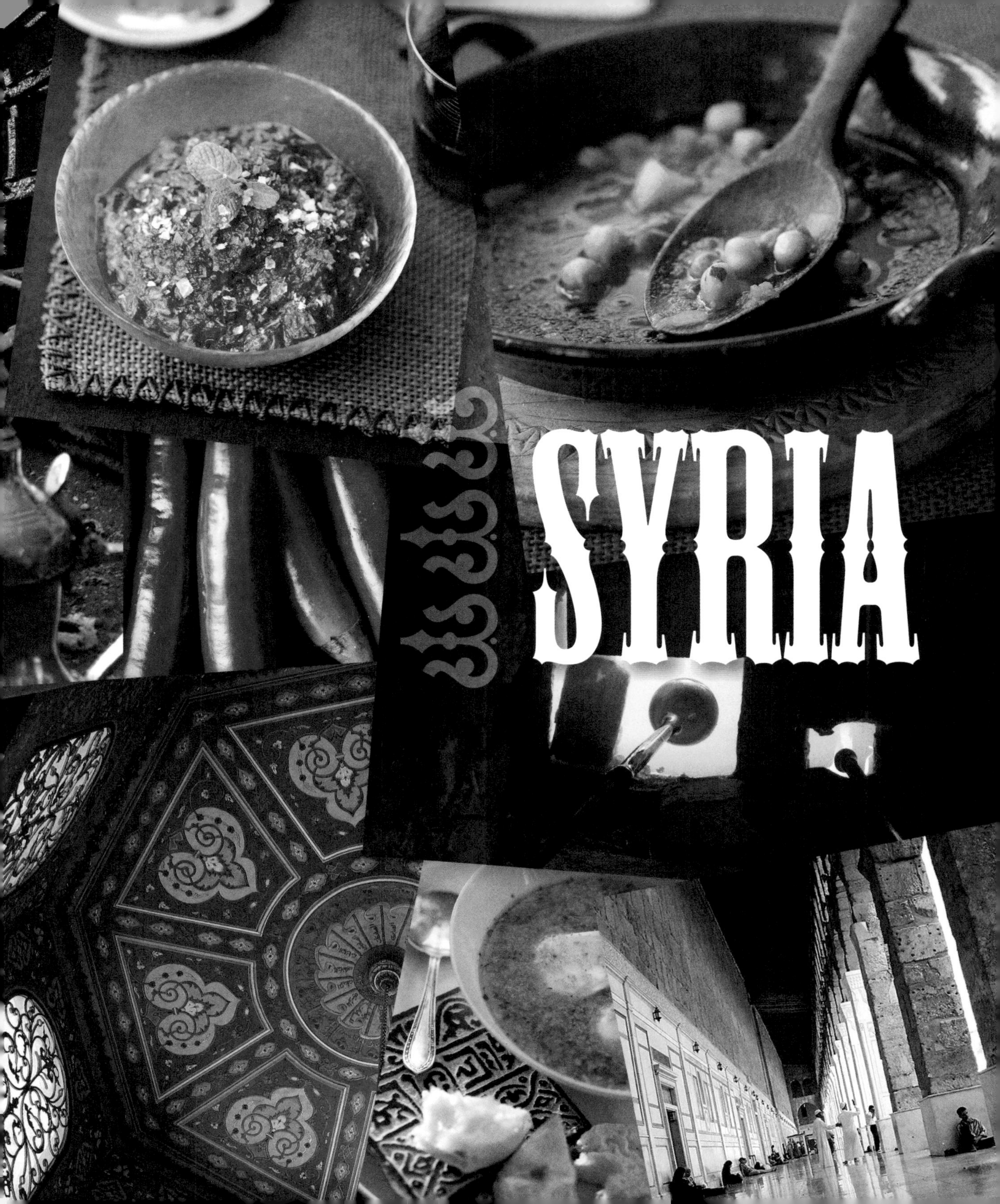
SYRIA

Syria

Syria is truly remarkable; its history so rich and colourful. After studying religion at school and learning about John the Baptist, I never would have thought that one day I would be standing next to his tomb in a mosque in Damascus.

The people of Syria were warm and welcomed us with open arms, inviting us into their homes and into their hearts. The food—again—was everything it should be and deserves its high reputation. The traditional cuisine is varied and rich and often simply cooked. The variety of flavours and textures is so intriguing, leaving me with wonderful memories that even now stir the appetite. In Syria, the dining experience is all about sharing—different dishes are placed in the middle of the table and everyone helps themselves—a truly great way to eat.

Time either stands still or sweeps through like a sandstorm. In Syria I witnessed what is potentially the end of a nomadic way of life which stretches back into the mists of time, and also saw the permanence of history built in stone. Driving into Palmyra was like being on a movie set with all its extraordinary ruins; it was an amazing experience to walk right up to them and touch these structures, without the barriers that we have become so used to in the West. Surrounded by this rich history, I marvelled at human ingenuity, enjoyed the company of good people and tasted some unforgettable food and coffee.

I am humbled by the remarkable journey that I have been so fortunate to take. The discoveries I made and the people I have met will remain in my memory forever. I hope you enjoy the journey as much as I have—remember it is just a glimpse of some amazing places, people and food. The only way to fully understand it is to discover it for yourself. Life is too short to be the victim of fanatics. Take the journey.

Old Damascus

Damascus is where it's said all journeys, civilizations and religions begin and end. And it's no exaggeration to say that much of what we know as the modern cosmopolitan world first saw the light of day in Damascus. Trade, which started as early as 8000 BC, brought people, goods and ideas from other cultures, fuelling a great forward movement into what we now call civilization. 'The cheque is in the mail' was probably first uttered in Damascus. The word 'cheque' is Arabic in origin, and the now-familiar concept was invented twelve centuries ago by traders plying this route.

Saint Paul's conversion on the road to Damascus, when he was struck blind by a vision, is a well-known story. But Damascus is also where he escaped a grisly fate. The Saint's habit of preaching Christianity in the synagogues of Damascus made him very unpopular. There was a plot by the Jews to kill him, but he escaped, it is said, lowered in a basket through a window in the city wall. Saint Paul lived to preach another day.

Damascus is also the final resting place of Kane, the first Son. His bones are said to have been safeguarded here since the dawn of time. It's also where the honourable military genius Saladin is entombed. He is considered the greatest Arab leader in history, having united the Arab world in order to expel the Crusaders.

Syria is a land of myths, legends and fables, with tales of heroic deeds, crusader knights and noble quests. To learn more about its rich history and many stories there's only one man who can regularly bring them to life. Rashid Shadi is probably the last member of the centuries-old tradition of *hakawati* or storytellers. Each night in Damascus, he breathes life into classic Arabian epics with enormous passion. He takes his place in his well-worn storyteller's chair in the Nawfara Café, as it gradually begins to fill with people ordering small cups of thick, black Syrian coffee or cups of tea. *Narghiles* (oriental tobacco water pipes) are packed, and the air is filled with a spicy aroma. There's no formality to this storytelling—the audience, who know these stories by heart, enthusiastically interject as each tale unfolds. Some stories take over a year to tell. The evening's entertainment will only end at the final call to prayer.

As in India and Morocco, sweets are important gifts in Syria. They are a social necessity and many occasions involve the offering of sweets. Births, marriages, business deals and holy days are times when only the best quality will do. Daoud Brothers is a company famous throughout the Arabic world, and their methods of production and presentation have become a fine art. Though sweet-making in Damascus goes back a very long way, Daoud Brothers and Co. was established in the early twentieth century. There are five brothers involved in the business, and they export all over the world. Even though it is a factory with amazingly modern equipment, nearly everything is done by hand. There are sixty or more proud sweet-makers, producing rack upon rack of tiny, intricate delicacies. To be a chef, you need passion and dedication, and I could see both in the faces of the people. The aroma of roasted sesame seeds, pistachios and other nuts was heavenly.

One of my personal favourite sweets is *barazek*. It's made with sweet pastry and toasted sesame seeds, and is moulded and baked in the oven. My other favourite is *namoura*, with layers of buttered filo pastry, filled with a delicate sheep's milk curd. I watched the whole sweet-making process through to the packing room, where these sweets were packed into lavishly decorated wooden boxes. Some of the boxes were even hand-carved. These Syrian sweet-makers definitely live up to their motto: 'A Taste from Heaven on Earth'.

But without a doubt the beating heart of Damascus is the Umayyad Mosque; the city's streets radiate outward from here. Based on its reputation as one of the wonders of the world, the prophet Mohammed refused to enter the gates, fearing it would spoil his ultimate entry into celestial heaven. What we see now was mostly built in the year 715, when Damascus was the capital of the Muslim Empire.

The ancient church that stood here, where both Christians and Muslims worshipped, was demolished, and the Christians were paid compensation. The head of John the Baptist, important for both religions, was found buried here during the building works; miraculously, it showed very little sign of decay.

The story goes that Herod sent the head here to prove to the Romans that John was dead. The Romans buried his head in an unmarked grave. The mosque has always been considered a sacred site. It was the Temple of Hadad, the Aramaean God of Storms, way back in 2000 BC. Later, in Roman times, it was known as the Temple of Jupiter. In the Byzantine era it was a Christian church dedicated to John the Baptist. Unlike in Morocco, not only was I allowed to enter the mosque, but also to witness, up close, a very special part of daily worship: the call to prayer. It was a moment I'll never forget.

SERVES 6

36 natural oysters, on the half-shell
1 pomegranate
150 g (5½ oz) unsalted butter
2½ tablespoons lemon juice
2 garlic cloves, crushed
1 handful flat-leaf (Italian) parsley, finely chopped
½ medium telegraph (long) cucumber, peeled and cut into thin, small sticks

Oysters with Pomegranates. Fresh, natural oysters are a great way to start a meal. While they taste wonderful with just a squeeze of fresh lemon juice or a dash of flavoured vinegar, in this recipe I have added a Syrian-inspired twist.

Forget using cutlery to eat fresh oysters, they are best eaten straight from the shell to savour the natural taste of the sea and the sweet flavour of the oyster itself.

Carefully remove the oysters from their shells and place them in a bowl. Rinse the shells and wipe them clean with paper towel. Set aside.

Cut the pomegranate in half and push the skin so the seeds pop out. Using your fingers, pick out any remaining seeds, removing the white pith. Reserve the seeds and discard the skin and pulp. Set aside until needed.

Heat the butter in a saucepan over low–medium heat for 1 minute, or until it starts to turn a nutty brown colour. Remove from the heat, making sure it doesn't burn. Add 1½ tablespoons lemon juice—the mixture will start to bubble. Allow it to settle, then pass through a fine sieve.

In a separate bowl, mix the garlic, the remaining lemon juice and parsley together. Add the warm butter mixture and stir to combine.

Space the oyster shells out evenly on a serving plate. Spoon a small amount of the cucumber into each shell and place an oyster on top. Spoon about 5 pomegranate seeds on each oyster, then drizzle a teaspoon of the garlic lemon dressing over the top and serve immediately.

SERVES 4

1 garlic bulb, plus 1 crushed garlic clove, extra
1 teaspoon vegetable oil
60 ml (2 fl oz/¼ cup) olive oil
400 g (14 oz) tin cannellini beans, rinsed and drained
2 tablespoons red wine vinegar
4 tablespoons extra virgin olive oil, plus extra, to serve
finely grated zest of 1 lime
1½ tablespoons lime juice
sea salt and freshly ground black pepper, to taste
120 g (4¼ oz) soft creamy feta cheese, crumbled
1 handful pitted black olives, roughly chopped

Bean Dip with Feta. In Syria dips are served at almost every meal and the varieties are endless. This one has a unique combination of flavours that marry well together—the texture of the beans finished with the saltiness of the feta and olives comes together perfectly. It can be served hot or cold.

Peel away the outer layers of the garlic bulb skin, leaving the skins of the individual cloves intact. With a knife, cut off 5–6 mm (¼ inch) from the top of the bulb, exposing the individual cloves of garlic.

Place the garlic bulb, with skin on, in a small roasting tray. Drizzle with the vegetable oil and a pinch of salt, making sure it is well coated. Cover with foil and bake for 30 minutes, or until the cloves feel soft when pressed. Remove from the oven and allow to cool. Cut the skin slightly around the cloves and peel. Set aside.

Heat the olive oil in a large saucepan over low heat. Add the extra crushed garlic and stir for 2 minutes, or until aromatic. Add the beans and vinegar and cook for a further 5 minutes, or until all the liquid is absorbed. Remove from the heat and allow to cool slightly before transferring to a food processor. Add the roast garlic, extra virgin olive oil, lime zest and lime juice. Blend until smooth and season well.

To serve, fold in the feta cheese and olives, place in a bowl and drizzle with a litte extra virgin olive oil.

SERVES 6

100 ml (3½ fl oz) olive oil
finely grated zest of 1 lemon
2½ tablespoons lemon juice
4 garlic cloves, crushed
2 teaspoons cayenne pepper
30 chicken wings
1 small handful coriander (cilantro) leaves, finely chopped
sea salt and freshly ground black pepper, to taste

Chicken Wings with Cayenne and Coriander. In Syria, a lot of the mezze included chicken wings. This is a great, simple dish to create and really messy to eat—which is part of the fun.

In a large non-metallic bowl, mix the olive oil, lemon zest, lemon juice, garlic and cayenne pepper and stir to combine. Add the chicken wings and toss to coat all over. Cover with plastic wrap and refrigerate for 3 hours in the marinade.

Preheat the oven to 200°C (400°F/Gas 6).

Put the wings on a baking tray in a single layer and cook in the oven for 20 minutes, turning a couple of times; the wings should be golden brown on all sides and cooked through. Remove from the oven, cover with foil and rest for 5 minutes.

Transfer to a bowl and toss through the chopped coriander. Season to taste and serve immediately.

SERVES 6

Hummus
500 g (1 lb 2 oz) tin chickpeas, rinsed and drained
4 tablespoons tahini
3½ tablespoons lemon juice
6 garlic cloves, crushed
125 ml (4 fl oz/½ cup) extra virgin olive oil

4 x 100 g (3½ oz) lamb fillets
20 g (¾ oz) sumac (see glossary)
60 ml (2 fl oz/¼ cup) olive oil

Hummus with Fried Lamb and Sumac. Hummus is always popular, and in Syria they serve it with fried lamb rolled in sumac as an entrée.

To make the hummus, blend the chickpeas in a food processor until smooth. Mix in the tahini, lemon juice, garlic and extra virgin olive oil. Season well with salt and stir to combine.

To prepare the lamb, roll the lamb fillets well in the sumac, making sure they are coated all over. Season well with salt.

Heat the olive oil in a frying pan over medium heat. Cook for 2½ minutes on each side to seal. The lamb will still be quite pink, if you prefer it well cooked, then cook for a further 1 minute on each side. Remove from the heat, cover, and rest in a warm place for 5 minutes, before cutting into thin slices.

To serve, spoon the hummus onto a large platter. Arrange the lamb slices over the top. Season with a little sumac and salt and serve with Moroccan Bread (see recipe, page 137).

SERVES 4

35 g (1¼ oz/¼ cup) wholemeal (whole-wheat) flour
435 g (15¼ oz/3½ cups) plain (all-purpose) flour, plus extra, for rolling
2 teaspoons fresh yeast
2 teaspoons sugar
2 tablespoons olive oil
1 small brown onion, finely chopped
1 teaspoon ground cinnamon
300 g (10½ oz) minced (ground) lamb
4 tablespoons tomato sauce (see recipe, page 216)
4 balls buffalo mozzarella
2 large sprigs oregano, leaves picked

Cinnamon Lamb Pizza with Oregano. While in Damascus we discovered a remarkable bakery. They made these wonderful little pizzas freshly baked in the wood-fired oven. We went back there many times because they tasted so wonderful.

To make the pizza bases, place the flours, yeast, sugar and 2½ teaspoons salt into a mixer with a dough hook. With the motor running, slowly add 420 ml (14½ fl oz/1⅔ cups) water and 2 teaspoons of the oil. Leave the mixer on a low speed for 10 minutes, or until a smooth, firm dough forms.

Divide the dough into four even portions, place on a lightly oiled tray and cover with a damp tea towel (dish towel). Leave for about 2 hours, or until the dough has doubled in size.

Roll out each portion onto a lightly floured surface to create four circles that have a 12 cm, (4½ in) diameter and are 5 mm (¼ in) thick. Preheat the oven to 220°C (425°F/Gas 7).

Heat the remaining oil in a frying pan over medium heat. Add the onion and cinnamon and fry for about 2–3 minutes, or until the onion is soft. Add the lamb and cook for 20–30 minutes, or until it is crispy. Make sure you keep stirring the mince to break it down into small pieces. Remove from the pan and drain on paper towel.

Place the pizza bases on baking trays. Spread 1 tablespoon of tomato sauce over each one, spreading all the way to the edge. Sprinkle the lamb evenly over each base, then tear the buffalo mozzarella over the lamb. Bake in the oven for 10–15 minutes, or until the cheese has melted and the pizza bases are golden and crispy. Remove from the oven and sprinkle with the oregano. Season and serve immediately.

SERVES 6

Truffles
4 black Syrian truffles
1 lemon, sliced
1 garlic clove
2 flat-leaf (Italian) parsley sprigs
1 thyme sprig

1 kg (2 lb 4 oz) minced (ground) beef
1 handful flat-leaf (Italian) parsley, finely chopped
2 red onions, finely chopped
2 garlic cloves, finely chopped
1½ teaspoons baharat (see recipe, page 214)
olive oil, for brushing
6 pitta breads, cut in half
1 cos (romaine) lettuce, shredded
½ medium telegraph (long) cucumber, finely diced
4 tomatoes, diced
4 spring onions (scallions), thinly sliced
2 lemons, cut into wedges
sea salt, to taste

Ground Beef Kebabs with Syrian Truffles. Now, the last place I expected to see truffles was in Syria. I was especially surprised to find out they grow in the desert. Desert truffles are a distant relative of the mushroom family and are related to their more costly European cousins. The Bedouin scour the sands east of Damascus looking for the telltale cracks and grasses indicating that these luscious delicacies lie waiting beneath the surface.

Put the truffles, lemon, garlic, herbs and 500 ml (17 fl oz/2 cups) water in a saucepan over medium heat. Bring to the boil, reduce the heat and simmer for 5 minutes. Remove from the heat and set aside for 30 minutes to finish the cooking process, then drain.

Meanwhile, combine the beef, parsley, onion, garlic, baharat and 1 teaspoon salt in a food processor and blend until the mixture is smooth. Then, using your hands, knead the mixture for a few minutes to help blend the flavours together.

Take 2 tablespoons of the mix at a time and, using wet hands, mould it evenly around a skewer. (Soak bamboo skewers first to prevent them burning during cooking.) Repeat with the remaining mixture until you have 12 kebabs. Set aside for 15 minutes.

Heat a barbecue hotplate or frying pan to medium. Brush the kebabs lightly with oil and cook for 15 minutes, turning constantly, or until golden brown all over and cooked through.

Place the lettuce, cucumber, tomato and spring onion in the pitta bread halves, slipping the meat off the skewers and into the bread pockets. Thinly shave the truffles over the top. Add a squeeze of lemon juice and season before serving.

SERVES 4–6

3 tablespoons olive oil
1 teaspoon brown mustard seeds
1 large brown onion, finely chopped
3 garlic cloves, crushed
3 teaspoons smoked paprika
1 teaspoon turmeric
500 g (1 lb 2 oz) minced (ground) lamb
250 ml (9 fl oz/1 cup) dry white wine
250 g (9 oz) rigatoni
100 g (3½ oz/⅓ cup) plain yoghurt
150 g (5½ oz/1 cup) feta cheese, crumbled
sea salt and freshly ground black pepper, to taste

Spiced Lamb with Rigatoni and Feta. One night in Damascus after a long day's filming we decided to eat in at our hotel's restaurant. I had this pasta dish, which went down well with a cold Syrian beer. The chef said it was a Syrian dish that his mother made him. I'm not quite sure how authentic it is, but it tastes great.

Heat 2 tablespoons of the olive oil in a frying pan over medium heat. Add the mustard seeds and fry for 1–2 minutes, or until they start to pop. Add the onion and garlic and cook gently for 5 minutes, or until the onion is soft. Add the paprika and turmeric and keep stirring for about 2 minutes to release the flavours. Add the lamb mince, breaking it up with the back of a spoon to break up any large lumps. Cook for 5 minutes, or until the lamb starts to brown. Add the white wine and continue cooking for 8 minutes, or until the wine has evaporated and the lamb is golden brown.

Meanwhile, cook the pasta in a saucepan of boiling salted water with the remaining olive oil for about 7–10 minutes, or until *al dente*. Drain and rinse briefly under cold running water to rinse off any excess starch, then drain again.

Put the pasta in a large serving bowl. Add the yoghurt and crumbled feta to the pasta and mix well so that the yoghurt coats the pasta and the feta melts. Add the lamb and stir thoroughly. Season to taste and serve immediately.

SERVES 6

45 g (1½ oz/¼ cup) rice flour
750 ml (26 fl oz/3 cups) full-cream (whole) milk
125 g (4½ oz) caster (superfine) sugar
80 g (2¾ oz/¾ cup) ground almonds
1 tablespoon rosewater
pistachio nuts, to garnish
pomegranate seeds, to garnish

Muhallabia—Almond Pudding.

This was a popular dessert at Becash, an ice cream parlour in Damascus. The place was full from morning to night, and after tasting this wonderful delight I could truly understand why.

Mix the rice flour with 60 ml (2 fl oz/¼ cup) of the milk and set aside.

Put the remaining milk in a saucepan over medium-high heat and bring to the boil. Add the rice flour and milk mixture, sugar and a pinch of salt and stir until the sugar has dissolved. Reduce the heat and simmer, stirring constantly, for 5 minutes, or until the mixture thickens slightly. Stir in the ground almonds and rosewater, remove from the heat and allow to cool for about 1 hour. (The mixture will thicken further to a soft rice pudding consistency.)

Pour the muhallabia into individual bowls and garnish with the pistachios and pomegranate seeds, to serve.

Bedouins, Crusaders and Giant Waterwheels

The word 'Bedouin' is Arabic for 'desert wanderer'. In recent times these people's lives have undergone change, but one element remains constant—their overwhelming hospitality, which is famous throughout the world. Originally from the Persian Gulf, the Bedouin arrived in Syria before recorded time and now range as far west as the North African shores of the Mediterranean and the Atlantic coast of the Sahara.

Many early travellers on the caravan routes owed their lives to Bedouin generosity. Thousands of years spent scratching out a living in harsh conditions made the Bedouin invaluable companions if you were travelling the trade routes. But there were also some Bedouin who were infamous for raiding any caravan that crossed their path, so it was wise to hire them as guides.

In Syria today there are Bedouin who rule wealthy oil states, and remarkably, there are still families living a traditional nomadic life. Even though they have survived on very little for a very long time, ongoing droughts in recent times are making it increasingly difficult for these tribes to exist in a traditional way.

I was honoured to be invited into the home of Masloub and his family of ten children. His immediate family live in a tent compound, plus there are another 100 members of the family camped within a stone's throw. Their main source of income is livestock, and they slaughtered a sheep in my honour.

While the men sat around talking and listening to music, the women were busy preparing a Bedouin feast called *mansaf*. This included a lamb dish usually made for special occasions. The meat is cut into pieces and boiled in a large pot for a couple of hours with half a dozen herbs and spices. A range of small salads are prepared, and vermicelli is fried in butter to be used as a garnish. While the meat is boiling away, the host begins the age-old coffee ceremony known as *gahwa* (see page 190). This ritualized coffee preparation is mesmerizing to watch—it is as though the ceremony itself somehow enhances the flavour.

Once the coffee was consumed, it was time to serve up the *mansaf*. Boiled rice and almonds were put into a large pan and the lamb was placed on top, followed by the head, liver and eyeballs!

All the delicacies were carefully arranged and offered to the guest (in this instance, me) first. Everyone had gathered around in a circle as the feast was brought in. I was closely watched to make sure everything was to my satisfaction. The meat was tender and sweet (luckily someone else opted for the eyeballs). The boiled fat, however, was definitely an acquired taste.

Until recent decades the Bedouin followed a circuit of grazing lands that crossed national borders. Now everyone needs a passport and many Bedouin have been living in houses with solid walls.

A severe drought from 1958 to 1961 is said to have been the straw that broke the camel's back, so to speak. Many nomadic families were forced to settle, begin growing crops and learn a new way of life. They became known as the *fellahin*, which is the Bedouin name for families who settle in one place. I was honoured to glimpse an ancient nomadic culture that may not exist for very much longer.

Syria is not only home to the Bedouins but also known for the famous Krak des Chevaliers in the rural centre of Hama, one of the best preserved Crusader strongholds. It was built by the Arabs in a highly strategic location, and sits 650 metres (2132 feet) above sea level on a mountain, guarding the corridor called the Homs Gap, between Syria and the Mediterranean.

Its position is what made it so very important to the Crusader Knights. The bastion we see today was built in the eleventh century, on top of previous fortifications.

After its capture by the Crusaders, the castle was strengthened and extended by the Knights Hospitallers, a monastic order of warriors. In the twelfth century, they began building what we see today. The engineering was so good that even the great Saladin realized it was impregnable after only one day—the Crusader Knights saw that the construction and engineering was way ahead of anything they had yet seen, and took this knowledge with them back to Europe.

It wasn't until I entered the castle that I fully realized its incredible size and strength—until the invention of gunpowder it was virtually impregnable. Everywhere you look, it is in almost perfect condition, but minus the neighing of horses and the rattling of armour.

Everything is on a grand scale—there are thirteen huge towers, giving uninterrupted views of any threatening force days before it could arrive. Inside the walls was a pocket-sized town complete with a church, aqueducts, large halls and courtyards, vast stables, living quarters and well-stocked storerooms.

One story goes that in 1271 an Arab army laid siege on Krak des Chevaliers. Realizing a front-on attack was impossible, the Arab

Commander resorted to a simple trick—he forged a letter from the commander of the Infidels, instructing the knights to abandon their fortress and return home.

Whether or not this story is true, the Crusaders occupied the castle for over one-and-a-half centuries. When the castle was finally captured, they found the knights had enough food stored there to last them for up to five years.

Hama itself has retained much of its historic charm; as well as being a market town for the surrounding districts it is also the site of other engineering marvels.

Fresh water is the key ingredient for the establishment of any civilization and, historically, the Byzantines or 'Eastern Romans' devised a radical solution to supply fresh water to Hama. The banks of the river Orontes are very deep, so it was necessary to raise the water level several metres in order to supply water to the surrounding land. They achieved this in a very ingenious way.

The magnificent giant waterwheels or *norias* of Hama have been turning since the thirteenth century. The largest of the *norias* is a whopping 20 metres (65 feet) in diameter. And, though they've been replaced piece by piece over the years, the *norias* look exactly as they did when they were first built. By directing water through a system of elevated channels and aqueducts, it was possible for people to irrigate the surrounding land. The noise of groaning wood sounds like a symphony of chainsaws, but it must have been music to a farmer's ears all those years ago.

Though they're now relics of the past, seventeen of these ancient *norias* still continue to turn. In the age of electric pumps, Hama is still a major centre for agriculture and even aquaculture.

MAKES APPROXIMATELY 6 TABLESPOONS

5 tablespoons ground sumac (see glossary)
2 teaspoons dried thyme leaves
1 teaspoon cumin seeds
½ teaspoon paprika

Syrian Za'atar. Za'atar is a Middle Eastern spice blend based on Syrian Hyssop, a herb referenced in the Bible. It grows wild in the region and is similar to marjoram or oregano. This spice mix is the same as I experienced in Damascus. It was served on some flatbread that had been smeared with olive oil and sprinkled with this remarkable spice, then baked in the oven. Za'atar can also be mixed with olive oil and used as a dip for bread, or to season meat, kebabs and vegetables.

Grind together the sumac, thyme and cumin seeds using a mortar and pestle or coffee grinder, until you have a fine powder. Mix together with the paprika and ¼ teaspoon salt.

Syrian Za'atar will keep for 3 months stored in an airtight container.

SERVES 6

3 garlic cloves, crushed
9 large red capsicums (peppers), roasted and peeled (see recipe, page 215)
3 small red chillies, seeded and chopped
375 g (13 oz/3 cups) roughly chopped walnuts
55 g (2 oz/⅔ cup) fresh breadcrumbs, lightly toasted
3 tablespoons pomegranate molasses (see glossary)
5 tablespoons lemon juice
1½ teaspoons caster (superfine) sugar
185 ml (6 fl oz/¾ cup) extra virgin olive oil
sea salt and freshly ground black pepper, to taste

Red Capsicum Dip. This is one of my favourite dips—the flavour is perfect. Don't wash the capsicums after you have roasted them, or you'll wash away a lot of the flavour.

Mash together the garlic with 2 teaspoons salt until it forms a paste.

Roughly chop the capsicums and place in a food processor with the garlic paste, chilli, walnuts, breadcrumbs, pomegranate molasses, lemon juice and sugar. Season with salt and pepper and then blend until the mixture is pulpy. With the motor still running, slowly add the oil until the dip is thick and creamy. Season to taste and serve with toasted flatbread.

Capsicum dip will keep for up to 4 days stored in an airtight container in the refrigerator.

SERVES 4

800 g (1 lb 12 oz) watermelon, peeled and diced into 2 cm (¾ in) cubes, seeds removed
250 g (9 oz/1⅔ cups) crumbled soft creamy feta cheese
24 pitted black olives
10 fresh mint leaves, thinly sliced
finely grated zest of 2 limes
3 tablespoons lime juice
60 ml (2 fl oz/¼ cup) extra virgin olive oil
sea salt and freshly ground black pepper, to taste

Watermelon, Feta and Olive Salad. If I had my way, I would have a salad with lunch and dinner every day. Not only are salads very refreshing, but the acidity helps you digest the meal, especially if meat has been on the menu.

Put the watermelon, feta and olives in a large serving bowl.

Put the mint, lime zest, lime juice and olive oil in a jar with a lid. Shake to combine well. Pour the dressing over the salad and gently toss to coat. Season, to taste, and serve immediately.

COFFEE FOR THE SOUL

A cornerstone of Bedouin hospitality is the *gahwa*, a traditional age-old coffee ceremony that is still practised today. The ritual begins with the host roasting the coffee beans in a long-handled iron pan called a *mahmasa*, over an open flame. Once cooked, the beans are cooled and pulverized with a large wooden mortar and pestle called a *mahbash*. It's necessary to strike the side of the mortar occasionally to prevent the grounds from sticking together—this has developed into something of a musical art form—the grinder becomes a percussionist.

The thick black coffee is sometimes mixed with ground cardamom seeds and a pinch of saffron. It is the host's role to serve his guests small cups of the strong brew (if there is any doubt about who is the most important person in the room then the oldest is served first) and it is considered impolite to refuse the first cup. It is said the *gahwa* ceremony involves three cups of coffee: one for the soul, one for the sword and one for the guest.

SERVES 6

500 g (1 lb 2 oz) English spinach, rinsed, stems trimmed and roughly chopped
100 ml (3½ fl oz) olive oil
1 brown onion, finely chopped
½ teaspoon ground allspice
1 tablespoon sumac (see glossary)
salt and freshly ground black pepper, to taste
250 g (9 oz) soft creamy feta cheese
400 g (14 oz) ready-made puff pastry sheets

Spinach and Feta Fatayer. A fatayer is a type of pie that is commonly served in Syria. The flavour combination of the feta, spinach and spices is very addictive. I ate these regularly as a daytime snack throughout Syria.

Preheat the oven to 180°C (350°F/Gas 4). Lightly grease two baking trays.

Put the spinach, with just the water clinging to the leaves, in a frying pan over medium heat. Cook for 3–4 minutes, or until the spinach is wilted. Remove from the heat, allow to cool slightly and squeeze out the excess moisture from the spinach leaves.

Heat the oil in a frying pan over medium heat. Add the onion and cook for 10 minutes, or until golden brown. Add the spinach, allspice and sumac and season well. Make sure all the ingredients are thoroughly combined, then carefully fold in the feta so it doesn't break up too much.

Cut the pastry into twelve 10 cm (4 in) rounds with a pastry cutter.

Working with one round of pastry at a time, lay it flat in the palm of your hand. Put 1 tablespoon of the spinach and feta mixture in the centre. To make a traditional three-sided pie, join two edges together on one side of the circle, lifting over the filling and making a thin-ridged joint to seal. Lift the remaining open edge up and pinch firmly together to create a pyramid shape with a rounded base. Repeat this process with all the remaining pastry rounds and filling.

Place the pies on the prepared trays and bake for 25–30 minutes, or until the fatayer are golden brown on the outside and the cheese is melted in the middle. Serve hot.

SERVES 6

1 tablespoon olive oil
500 g (1 lb 2 oz) lamb, cut into 2 cm (¾ in) dice
1 brown onion, finely chopped
4 garlic cloves, crushed
½ teaspoon freshly grated nutmeg
½ teaspoon ground cinnamon
3 tablespoons lemon juice
375 ml (13 fl oz/1½ cups) chicken stock
50 g (1¾ oz/¼ cup) dried apricots, soaked in warm water
60 g (2¼ oz/½ cup) raisins
salt and freshly ground black pepper, to taste

Syrian Lamb and Apricot Stew. This is a simple stew and, typically for the area, it has a sweeter flavour because of the dried fruit. I recommend that you make this dish the day before you wish to serve it because, like all casseroles, the flavour is enhanced if left overnight.

Heat the oil in a heavy-based saucepan over medium–high heat. Add the lamb and cook, stirring, for 6–8 minutes, or until brown on all sides. Add the onion and garlic and cook for 2–3 minutes, or until the onion is soft. Add the nutmeg, cinnamon and lemon juice and cook for 2 minutes to allow the flavours to infuse.

Add the chicken stock, increase the heat and bring to the boil. Reduce the heat, cover the pan and simmer slowly for 1 hour, or until the meat is just starting to become tender.

Drain the apricots and add them to the pan with the raisins and 100 ml (3½ fl oz) water. Stir through and simmer for a further 20 minutes, or until the lamb is very tender. Skim off any scum that rises to the surface. Season to taste and serve immediately.

SERVES 4

800 g (1 lb 12 oz) minced (ground) lamb
1 red onion, finely chopped
3 garlic cloves, crushed
1 teaspoon ground cumin
1 teaspoon ground coriander
1 teaspoon paprika
1 small handful flat-leaf (Italian) parsley, chopped
1 small handful oregano, chopped
3 tablespoons olive oil
sea salt and freshly ground black pepper, to taste
8 small pitta breads, to serve
1 baby cos (romaine) lettuce, shredded
4 roma (plum) tomatoes, sliced
harissa (see recipe, pages 214–15), to serve

Lamb Kefta. Keftas are ground lamb kneaded together with onion, garlic, herbs and spices. They are very popular in Syria—unlike many kebabs where the meat can be sometimes a little tough, keftas are very tender and flavoursome.

Put the lamb mince, onion, garlic, spices, herbs and olive oil in a large mixing bowl. Knead very well with your hands, ensuring that everything is mixed thoroughly and the mince is quite smooth. Season well.

Using wet hands, divide the mixture into 8 even-sized portions and mould onto 8 skewers in long sausage shapes. (If using bamboo skewers, soak in cold water for a couple of hours first to prevent them burning during cooking.)

Preheat a barbecue hotplate or frying pan to medium. Cook, turning regularly, for 15 minutes, or until golden brown on both sides and cooked through.

Pull the meat from the skewers and serve inside the pitta bread with the lettuce, tomato and a dash of harissa.

SERVES 6

100 ml (3½ fl oz) white vinegar
1.2 kg (2 lb 12 oz) honeycomb tripe, cleaned (ask your butcher to do this for you)
100 g (3½ oz) soft brown sugar
100 ml (3½ fl oz) extra virgin olive oil
10 garlic cloves, crushed
12 French shallots, cut into quarters
1 small fennel bulb, thinly sliced
2 celery sticks, thinly sliced
2 noomi (dried limes) (see glossary)
2 teaspoons baharat (see recipe, page 214)
8 roma (plum) tomatoes, peeled (see method, page 215) and diced
150 ml (5 fl oz) white wine
50 ml (1¾ fl oz) white wine vinegar
1 litre (35 fl oz/4 cups) chicken stock
4 granny smith apples, peeled, cored and diced
400 g (14 oz) tin chickpeas, rinsed and drained
120 g (4¼ oz/¾ cup) peas
1 tablespoon red wine vinegar
salt and freshly ground black pepper, to taste
1 handful chopped flat-leaf (Italian) parsley, to garnish

Braised Honeycomb Tripe. Walking through the souks is an unforgettable experience, affording many amazing sights. Seeing the offal stalls was quite interesting, as it is not often you get to see offal displayed like this. Tripe is one of those ingredients a lot of people shy away from, but this is a great recipe and worth a try!

Bring 3 litres (105 fl oz/12 cups) water and the vinegar to the boil in a large saucepan over high heat. Reduce the heat, add the tripe and simmer for 30 minutes. Drain and slice thinly. Set aside.

Put the sugar and 150 ml (5 fl oz) water in a saucepan over low heat and stir until the sugar dissolves. Continue cooking until the liquid starts to caramelize. Remove from the heat and set aside.

Heat the oil in a large frying pan over medium heat. Add the garlic and cook for 1 minute, then add the shallots, fennel, celery, noomi and baharat and cook, stirring, for about 2–3 minutes, to allow the flavours to develop. Add the reserved sugar syrup and tomatoes and stir well. Add the tripe and mix through to coat in the sauce.

Add the wine and white wine vinegar and simmer for about 10 minutes, or until the liquid is reduced by half. Pour in the stock, bring to the boil, then reduce the heat and simmer for about 25 minutes. Add the apples and chickpeas and cook, covered, for a further 20 minutes, or until the tripe is tender.

Finally, add the peas and cook for a further 5 minutes, or until tender. Add the red wine vinegar and season to taste. Mix in the chopped parsley and serve immediately.

Aleppo

The ancient city of Aleppo, or '*Halab*' in Arabic, vies with Damascus and Jericho for the title of 'the oldest city in the world'. It is surmounted by a massive citadel, which sits 50 metres (164 feet) above its rooftops.

Aleppo is the most spellbinding city in Syria, and as far back as medieval times it was a centre for European powers seeking a foothold in the mysterious East. As ideas from Europe and Asia gradually seeped into the city, the people of Aleppo adapted and took on a worldlier attitude.

The city has a long history of invasions, beginning over 4000 years ago with the Amorites. A lot of invaders and emissaries stayed, and today you can find the descendants of Turkish, Armenian, Kurdish, Jewish and Russian people here. Orthodox Christianity and Islam have lived side by side in Aleppo for well over 1200 years.

In the eleventh and again in the twelfth centuries, the Crusaders tried to overrun the city, but on both occasions they were unsuccessful. Realizing the city's strategic importance, the legendary Saladin assigned his own son as Governor after taking Aleppo in 1183. For a time Aleppo enjoyed a long period of relative peace; trade flourished and it became the largest and wealthiest city in Syria.

The bazaar is vast, though the streets themselves are small. Here you'll find vendors selling liquorice juice, a drink loved by all Syrians. It is made by allowing water to seep slowly through a cloth containing liquorice fibres, a process that takes hours.

Aleppo is also renowned for its cuisine, which is considered Syria's finest. Its variety is enriched by the diverse traditions and cultures that have inhabited the city in the past.

Local cooks serve tasty versions of kebab, *kibbe* (ground cracked wheat and lamb), *mezze* (appetizers), and the usual stuffed vegetables. A few of my favourites were *muhammara*, a spicy paste eaten like hummus but made from a renowned hot pepper, pomegranate juice and ground

walnuts. I also enjoyed a kebab in a sauce of stewed fresh cherries, called *kabab bi-karaz*, and *kibbe* made with sumac and quince.

These traditional dishes draw upon the wealth of the surrounding countryside, with its flocks of Awassi sheep—the fat-tailed Middle Eastern breed—and orchards of olive, nut and fruit trees. Aleppo's famous pistachios are also used in many sweets, rolled in dough and smothered with various syrups.

Aleppo would definitely be one of my favourite Middle Eastern cities, and is worth going out of your way to visit. And while you're there, visit a '*hammam*'—it's not simply a bathhouse, but offers a ritualistic cleansing for both body and soul.

SERVES 4–6

500 g (1 lb 2 oz) beetroot
500 g (1 lb 2 oz/2 cups) plain yoghurt
1 tablespoon tahini
1 garlic clove, crushed
½ teaspoon ground cumin
finely grated zest of 1 lemon
2 tablespoons lemon juice
sea salt and freshly ground black pepper, to taste
20 mint leaves, thinly sliced (optional)
extra virgin olive oil, for drizzling
6 pides (Turkish/flat breads), warmed, to serve

Beetroot and Yoghurt Dip. This popular Middle Eastern dip is colourful, and also very tasty.

Peel the beetroot and trim the ends. Cut into chunks and place in a saucepan of boiling salted water. Cook for 30–45 minutes, or until tender. Use the point of a sharp knife to test if the beetroot is cooked—the knife should slide through, but the beetroot should still be firm. Remove from the heat, drain and refresh under cold running water, then drain again.

When cool enough to handle, coarsely grate the beetroot into a mixing bowl, then fold in the yoghurt, tahini, garlic, cumin, lemon zest and juice. Season to taste, cover, and refrigerate for at least 2–3 hours until chilled.

To serve, fold in the sliced mint, if desired, and adjust the seasoning, to taste. Place in a serving bowl, drizzle with a little extra virgin olive oil and serve with warm pide.

SERVES 4

400 g (14 oz) tin chickpeas, drained and rinsed
185 g (6½ oz/¾ cup) plain yoghurt
¼ teaspoon ground cumin
1 teaspoon caster (superfine) sugar
2 long green chillies, seeded and finely chopped
1 small handful coriander (cilantro) leaves, roughly chopped

Chickpea and Yoghurt Salad. This is a superb salad. It can be simply eaten on its own with any Middle Eastern-style bread, or it can be served with grilled lamb kebabs.

Mix the chickpeas, yoghurt, ground cumin, sugar, chilli, coriander and 1 teaspoon salt in a bowl and stir to combine thoroughly. Adjust the seasoning if necessary, cover and refrigerate for at least 1 hour before serving.

SERVES 8

300 g (10½ oz/2½ cups) plain (all-purpose) flour, plus extra, for dusting
½ teaspoon sugar
1 tablespoon dried yeast
150 g (5½ oz/⅔ cup) plain yoghurt
3 tablespoons olive oil

Yoghurt Bread. This is a recipe I picked up in Damascus; with the addition of the yoghurt it has a unique flavour.

Sift the flour into a large mixing bowl with ½ teaspoon salt. In another small bowl, mix together the sugar, yeast and 60 ml (2 fl oz/ ¼ cup) warm water and leave the mixture to sit until it starts to bubble. In a third bowl, mix together the yoghurt and olive oil.

Make a well in the flour and add the yeast mixture and yoghurt and oil. Mix to combine and once it has come together, use clean hands to knead for 10 minutes, or until the dough becomes smooth and elastic. Cover with a damp tea towel (dish towel) and leave in a warm place for about 1½–2 hours, or until the dough doubles in size.

Preheat the oven to 190°C (375°F/Gas 5). Divide the dough into 8 even-sized portions. Using the palm of your hand, push each portion out into a round disc with a 15 cm (6 in) diameter and about 1 cm (½ in) thick. Place on a lightly floured baking tray and bake in the oven for 15–20 minutes, or until a light golden brown and cooked through.

THE BAZAAR

In Aleppo, though the bazaar is vast, the streets are small and intimate compared to Damascus, with its massive thoroughfares. You can almost touch the roofs in the bazaar, which is a labyrinth of streets shooting off in all directions. It's exactly as I'd imagined the souks of the ancient world would have been—full of colour and charm, selling everything from antiques and clothing to jewellery stalls and of course, food.

The bazaars are a hub of daily life, bustling with people buying and selling their wares. The food smells that permeate the alleyways get your nose twitching and your belly rumbling with anticipation—each day I returned I discovered new and wonderful things to look at. You can find just about anything in the bazaars, from having your own scent of perfume made while you wait to ordering a suit made to measure—you just need to be ready to haggle!

SERVES 4

2 tablespoons white vinegar
4 large eggs
100 ml (3½ fl oz) olive oil
2 onions, finely chopped
7 garlic cloves, crushed
80 g (2¾ oz) butter
60 g (2¼ oz/¾ cup) breadcrumbs made from 3-day-old bread
1 handful coriander (cilantro) leaves, finely chopped
1.25 litres (44 fl oz/5 cups) chicken stock
1½ tablespoons red wine vinegar
sea salt and freshly ground black pepper, to taste

Garlic and Egg Soup. I walked into a little shop in Hama, in Syria, and all it sold was garlic. That was it—nothing else in sight. The aroma was divine.

I love garlic and use it a lot in my cooking. This soup is similar to something I had while in Hama, the difference being that they used hard-boiled eggs in theirs and here I have poached them.

To poach the eggs, bring a saucepan of water to the boil and add the vinegar. With a slotted spoon, stir the water in a clockwise direction. Crack the eggs into the water about 5 seconds apart. The spinning water will form the shapes of the poached eggs. Cook for 3–5 minutes, or until the egg whites are set. Refresh in cold water and set aside until needed.

Heat the oil in a frying pan over medium heat. Gently cook the onion for about 5 minutes, or until softened. Add half the crushed garlic and cook for a further 10 minutes, making sure the onion doesn't brown. Set aside and keep warm.

In another frying pan, melt the butter over low heat and gently cook the breadcrumbs stirring regularly for 8 minutes, or until golden brown. Remove from the pan and drain on paper towel.

Using a mortar and pestle, grind the coriander leaves with the remaining garlic and 2 teaspoons salt to make a smooth paste.

Heat the chicken stock in a large saucepan and bring to the boil. Add the red wine vinegar, then gently add the poached eggs to reheat for 1 minute. Carefully remove the eggs with a slotted spoon and place in the base of a large serving bowl.

Add the onion and the coriander paste to the stock and stir through. Adjust the seasoning, to taste, then ladle the soup over the poached eggs. Sprinkle with the breadcrumbs and serve immediately.

SERVES 4

125 g (4½ oz/1 cup) plain (all-purpose) flour
250 g (9 oz/1 cup) plain yoghurt
2 teaspoons caster (superfine) sugar
½ teaspoon ground fennel
¼ teaspoon ground cardamom
150 ml (5 fl oz) vegetable oil
300 g (10½ oz/2½ cups) goat's curd or soft white goat's cheese
good quality honey, to serve

Yoghurt Pancakes with Goat's Curd and Honey. This recipe is a version of a dish I tried in a restaurant in Aleppo. The cook stood over a very big hotplate just churning these pancakes out, all consistently good. He smothered one crumpet-like pancake with a little butter, then topped it with goat's curd and honey and passed it to me. Unfortunately, the crew wanted to share!

You need to start this recipe the day before, to allow the batter to settle and the flavours to infuse.

Sift the flour into a bowl and stir in the yoghurt. Add 60 ml (2 fl oz/¼ cup) water and stir until a smooth batter forms. Whisk in the sugar, fennel and cardamom. Cover with plastic wrap and refrigerate overnight.

The next day, whisk the batter again and stir in a pinch of salt. Heat the oil in a frying pan over medium heat. Pour about ½ cup of the batter into the pan at a time and swirl it around the base of the pan to make a thin pancake. Cook for 2 minutes on each side, or until golden brown. Gently remove the pancake from the pan and keep warm in a low-temperature oven. Repeat this process to make 8 pancakes in total.

Place 2 pancakes on a plate, add a spoonful of goat's curd and drizzle with honey, to serve.

GLOSSARY, BASICS, INDEX

Glossary

Ajowan seeds are from the herb ajowan, which is related to parsley and cumin. The seeds are teardrop shaped, and very pungent. Their taste is similar to that of the herb thyme. They are available from most Asian grocery stores.

Argan oil is the oil from the fruit of the argan tree and is a relative newcomer to Australia. The tree grows in Morocco and the very nutritious oil is extracted from the nuts of that tree. The argan tree is listed on UNESCO's World Heritage List. Argan oil is a little darker in colour than olive oil, and has a nutty taste. It is available from Middle Eastern grocery stores.

Curry leaves are picked from the deciduous curry tree, which is related to citrus. Don't confuse true curry leaves with those of another garden plant, the grey–silver curry plant. Curry leaves have a citrus aroma and add greatly to various curry spice blends. You can buy them fresh from the greengrocer or dried from Asian grocery stores.

Dal (also known as dhal) is the general name for the group of dried pulses (split peas, lentils, beans) that can be used to make the dish of the same name. Most often dal is made with yellow or red lentils, but the dish can be made with any dal.

Moong dal is the name for dried, split mung beans, and they are yellow in colour. Urad dal is a black-skinned lentil that is cream-coloured inside.

Demerara sugar is a brown sugar mixed with a little molasses. It is available in supermarkets.

Dosa is a pancake made from the flour of ground pulses. The batter is mixed and then usually left overnight. In the morning, the dosa batter is cooked, and various fillings are added.

Fenugreek leaves and seeds Fenugreek is a small, flowering herb and its seeds are a spice. The seeds are contained in the small, bean-shaped fruit of the plant. The seeds are small and golden in colour, and quite hard. They are highly aromatic. The leaves can be cooked and eaten, or dried and used as a flavouring, although they can be somewhat difficult to source. The seeds are available from Asian grocery stores and specialty stores where spices are sold.

Garam masala is an Indian spice blend featuring ground cumin, coriander, cardamom, cloves and nutmeg.

Gelatine leaves Leaf gelatine is available in sheets of varying sizes. Be careful to check the manufacturer's instructions regarding which ratio of liquid-to-gelatine sheet to use. If leaves are unavailable, use gelatine powder instead, making sure it is dissolved in warm liquid before use. Again, refer to the manufacturer's instructions when in doubt.

Harissa is a spice paste based on chillies. It can be extremely hot, depending on how it is made. Harissa is often used as a condiment, and can be served with cooked meats.

Moong dal—see Dal.

Muscovado sugar is a dark brown sugar that contains a lot of molasses. It is available in supermarkets and specialty food stores.

Mustard oil is oil pressed from mustard seeds. At room temperature, the flavour is not very strong, but the flavour increases as the oil is heated. Mustard oil is available from Asian grocery stores.

Nigella seeds come from a plant in the buttercup family. The seeds are small, black and teardrop shaped. There is a lot of confusion about nigella seeds, and they are often sold under incorrect names including black cumin or black onion seed. Buying spices from a knowledgeable and reputable dealer will ensure you end up with the correct spice.

Noomi is one of the names for dried limes. These are whole limes dried in the sun. The colour varies from pale brown to quite dark. The inside can be very black, and has a strong citrus aroma. Noomi can be found in specialty grocery stores and Asian grocery stores.

Pomegranate molasses is a dark, flavoursome molasses made from pomegranate juice cooked down with sugar and lemon. The resulting mix is thick and acidic, with a very sharp flavour. It is available in specialty food stores and is becoming more widely available.

Raita is a yoghurt-based dish served as a cooling side dish to curries and other spicy food. The yoghurt is often mixed with other ingredients, including cucumber and coconut.

Sumac is the powder ground from the berries of the sumac tree. It is a deep red-purple in colour and imparts a wonderful salty and fruity flavour. Sumac should be purchased from reputable dealers, to ensure you are using true culinary sumac, as some trees in the same botanical family can cause allergic reactions.

Tagine is a traditional Middle Eastern dish with a lid that can be used on the stovetop or in the oven. The conical shape of the tagine lid is designed to preserve moisture in food as it cooks by recirculating the moisture that condenses in the lid. If you buy a terracotta tagine, you will need to season it before cooking, unless it is frequently in use (see page 216). Tagine is also the name given to a dish prepared in the tagine.

Tamarind is the sour pulp of an Asian fruit. It is most commonly available compressed into cakes or refined as a concentrate in jars. Tamarind concentrate is widely available in supermarkets and Asian grocery stores.

Urad dal—see Dal.

Za'atar is the name given to a spice blend usually made from thyme, sumac and sesame seeds, although there are regional variations. Za'atar goes well with bread and can be used to season meat, kebabs and vegetables.

Basics

Baharat (makes 6 tablespoons)

Baharat is a mixture of spices and literally means spice in Arabic, which I am told is derived from the word '*bahar*' meaning 'pepper'.

2 tablespoons freshly ground black pepper
2 tablespoons ground cardamom
1 tablespoon ground cloves
1 tablespoon ground coriander
1 nutmeg, finely grated
1 pinch ground cinnamon

Mix all the ingredients together and store in an airtight container for up to 3 months.

Basmati Rice (serves 4)

200 g (7 oz/1 cup) basmati rice
1 tablespoon vegetable oil

Rinse the rice well under cold running water. Place in a heavy-based saucepan over medium heat with the oil, ¼ teaspoon salt and 375 ml (13 fl oz/1½ cups) water. Bring to the boil, then reduce the heat, cover with a tight-fitting lid and simmer for 10 minutes. Remove the lid and check that the rice is cooked—all the water should be absorbed. Fluff with a fork to separate any grains that are stuck together and serve immediately or use as required.

Chicken (Cutting into 8 Pieces)

Place the whole chicken, breast side up, on a chopping board. Hold one leg and pull it away from the body, cutting around the thigh to remove the leg and thigh. Cut into the joint between the thigh and drumstick to separate. Repeat on the other side. Pull the wing to the side and cut through the joint at the shoulder. Repeat on the other side. Using kitchen scissors, cut down the centre of the breast to separate the two breast fillets. Open the chicken out and cut either side of the backbone and remove it.

Couscous

Couscous is a tiny granulated pasta made from ground semolina, which is the hard part of the wheat grain. It is readily available in supermarkets. The commercial couscous we most often use today is precooked, so it only needs moistening with boiling water. The grains absorb the water and swell up. Cooking instructions are usually found on the packet.

Simply mix the necessary quantities of couscous and boiling water in a bowl, cover the bowl and allow to sit while the grains absorb the water. When the grain is ready—this usually only takes 5–10 minutes—you can add a little olive oil or butter to savoury couscous if you wish. Fluff the grains with a fork to separate. Generally allow for 185 g (6½ oz/1 cup) of couscous per person.

Garlic and Saffron Mayonnaise (serves 6–8)

This mayonnaise can be used with grilled or pan-fried fish, or served with a bowl of chips.

2 garlic cloves, crushed
pinch of saffron threads infused in 1 tablespoon hot fish stock or water
400 g (14 oz/1⅔ cups) mayonnaise
3 tablespoons lemon juice

In a mixing bowl, blend the garlic, drained saffron threads, mayonnaise and lemon juice.

Mix together, season with salt. Cover and chill for at least 3 hours before using to allow the flavours to infuse. Store in the refrigerator in a sterilized airtight jar for up to 3 days.

Harissa (makes 150 g/5½ oz/⅔ cup)

This is something every refrigerator should hold—simple to make, yet with so many uses. It can be used as a condiment to baste fish and meat, or as an ingredient in salads, or to spice up olives.

10 long red chillies, seeded and roughly chopped
3 garlic cloves
2 tablespoons lemon juice
2 tablespoons red wine vinegar
3 tablespoons olive oil
1 teaspoon cumin seeds, roasted and ground (see method, page 216)

Blend the chillies, garlic, lemon juice and vinegar together to form a thick paste. Fold in the oil, cumin and season well with salt. Store in a sterilized airtight jar in the refrigerator, and use as required. Harissa will keep for up to 4 weeks stored in an airtight container in the refrigerator.

Nuts, Toasted and Ground

Place the nuts in a small frying pan over low heat. Gently cook the nuts for 10 minutes, stirring constantly, or until golden brown. Watch the nuts carefully as you toast them—some nuts burn very quickly. Remove from the heat as soon as they have reached the desired colour. Once cooled, nuts can then be ground in a food processor.

Peeling Tomatoes

To peel tomatoes, first cut the core from the stem end using a sharp knife. Score a cross in the skin of the other end. Place the tomatoes in a saucepan of boiling water for about 30 seconds, or until the skin starts to peel. Remove and place in cold water briefly to cool. Drain, then gently peel away the skin with your hands.

The tomatoes can then be chopped and used as required. If the seeds are not to be used, simply scrape them out of the halved tomatoes with a teaspoon.

Ras el Hanout (makes 8 tablespoons)

The name itself translates to 'top of the shop', meaning that it is a blend of the best spices a seller can provide. Used in a variety of Moroccan dishes, the blends greatly vary and can have anything from 10 to 100 different spices.

2 tablespoons crushed black peppercorns
2 tablespoons crushed dried lavender
2 tablespoons crushed dried rosebuds
1 tablespoon ground turmeric
1 tablespoon ground cardamom
1 tablespoon ground mace
1 tablespoon ground ginger
1 teaspoon cayenne pepper
1 teaspoon crushed fennel seeds
1 teaspoon freshly grated nutmeg
1 teaspoon ground allspice
1 teaspoon ground cinnamon
4 cloves, crushed
1 pinch saffron threads

Place all the ingredients in a large mortar and pestle or spice grinder with 2 teaspoons salt and pound or blend until you have a smooth, fine powder. Store in an airtight container until ready to use. Ras el hanout will last for 3 weeks stored in an airtight container.

Roasting/Grilling and Peeling Capsicums (Peppers)

Preheat the oven to 200°C (400°F/Gas 6).

Cut the capsicums lengthways into large pieces. Lightly oil the capsicums and place, skin side up, in a baking tray. Place in the hottest part of the oven and cook for about 30 minutes, or until the skins are blackened.

Remove from the oven and place in a bowl. Cover the bowl with plastic wrap or a paper bag, making sure the top of the bowl is sealed. Leave to rest for 30–45 minutes (this softens the skins making them easier to remove).

Remove the capsicums from the bowl and peel the skins off with your fingers. Remove any remaining seeds. Do not wash them before or during peeling, as you will lose the natural oils and flavour. Use as required.

Spices, Roasted and Ground

Roasting spices enhances their flavour and gives the spice blend more strength. Roast spices work best with more robust, meaty dishes. Provided your spices are fresh, you may not wish to roast them if you are making a vegetable dish, as the vegetables don't require such strength of flavour.

Heat a frying pan over medium heat and add your spices to the pan. Dry-roast the spices for about 2 minutes, stirring constantly so that they don't burn. Once roasted, the spices can be ground or blended using a mortar and pestle or spice grinder.

Sterilizing Jars

Preheat the oven to 150°C (300°F/Gas 2).

Wash the jars thoroughly in hot soapy water, and rinse well. Alternatively, you can wash them in the dishwasher. While the jars are still hot, carefully place them and the lids on a tray and put them into the oven. Sterilize the jars in the oven for 30 minutes.

When hot liquid is poured into the jar and the lid is screwed on, invert the jar and leave to stand on a firm surface. This helps to sterilize the lid.

Tagines, and How to Season Them

Tagines are wonderful cooking pots. The conical shape of the tagine lid is designed to preserve moisture in food as it cooks by recirculating the moisture that condenses in the lid.

Some tagines available in homewares shops are purely decorative and should not be used for cooking at all; some can be used for serving, but should not be placed over heat. Check with the shop you purchase from, or the manufacturer.

Before using a terracotta tagine you need to season it first. Unless it is frequently in use it is a good idea to season the tagine each time you use it. To do this, soak it in water for at least 1 hour. Dry the tagine and rub olive oil over the inside of the base and lid. Place in a cold oven. Turn the oven to a temperature of 150°C (300°F/Gas 2). Leave the tagine in the oven for 1½ hours. Remove and allow to cool. Your tagine is now seasoned and ready for use.

Tomato Sauce (makes 1 litre/35 fl oz/4 cups)

60 ml (2 fl oz/¼ cup) olive oil
2 small brown onions, finely chopped
2 garlic cloves, finely chopped
5 kg (11 lb 14 oz) tomatoes, peeled, seeded and evenly chopped (see method, page 215)
15 basil leaves
salt and freshly ground black pepper, to taste

Heat the oil in a saucepan over low–medium heat and add the onion. Cook for 10 minutes, or until soft but not coloured. Add the garlic and cook for 2 minutes, then add the tomato and cook for 10 minutes, or until the tomato has softened. Add the basil and season, to taste.

Cover and cook over low heat for 1 hour, or until the sauce has thickened. Remove from the heat and allow to cool slightly, then transfer to a food processor and blend until smooth. Adjust the seasoning, to taste.

Transfer immediately into sterilized airtight jars (see method, opposite). Seal and allow to cool to room temperature. Tomato sauce will keep stored for 1 week in the refrigerator once opened.

Index

Acknowledgments

Thanks to: Mike Dickinson for all your support, sharing the dream, the walk in the Indian monsoon rain and an amazing adventure; Bob Grieve for your continued support, and everyone at Dreampool Productions; Bev Friend, our paths crossed again—many thanks for making this happen; Brent Love, what can I say, you are a legend—thanks for all your assistance with the photo shoot; Megan Chalmers, your loyal support has been truly appreciated, good luck in your new ventures and with parenthood; Anne Diplock, for all your support, especially when I was stressed out opening the restaurant—I couldn't have done it without you and you made it so much fun; Brendon—you're a part of this too and thank you; all my suppliers who have patiently supported me; Clare Green for all you did and with making the Feast Foundation happen and also Dan for your patience; Fiona, Helen and all my staff past and present at Véra—you all give so much to the Véra family and it means a lot to our customers and to me.

Juliet Rogers and Kay Scarlett at Murdoch Books—a very big thank you for giving me this amazing opportunity to work with a great team who really helped bring this book together, especially Jane Lawson and Reuben Crossman—Reuben you made it look amazing; Greg Elms for your photography and making the food look outstanding and creating a true visual 'Feast'; Georgia Young for adding your touch of style.

Also to David and Shaun—to a great future; it has been absolutely fabulous to meet you and know you, and looking forward to our new venture.

And finally I thank my wife, Wendy, and my beautiful son Jack—without your continued support and patience I couldn't do any of this. Thank you.x

Published in 2008 by Murdoch Books Pty Limited

Murdoch Books Australia
Pier 8/9, 23 Hickson Road
Millers Point NSW 2000
Phone: +61 (0) 2 8220 2000
Fax: +61 (0) 2 8220 2558
www.murdochbooks.com.au

Murdoch Books UK Limited
Erico House, 6th Floor
93–99 Upper Richmond Road
Putney, London SW15 2TG
Phone: +44 (0) 20 8785 5995
Fax: +44 (0) 20 8785 5985
www.murdochbooks.co.uk

Chief Executive: Juliet Rogers
Publishing Director: Kay Scarlett

Food editor: Jane Lawson
Editors: Tricia Dearborn, Jacqueline Blanchard
Concept and design: Reuben Crossman
Food photography: Greg Elms
Other photography: Michael Dickinson except: pp. 5, 8, 9, 39, 99, 113, 133, 149 (Alan Benson); cover and pp. 23, 48 (Getty Images); pp. 6, 10, 11, 93, 94, 95, 167, 210 (Istockphoto); and pp. 94, 162, 163, 198 (Stock.xchng)
Food stylist: Georgia Young
Production: Kita George

National Library of Australia Cataloguing-in-Publication Data
Véra, Barry.
Feast bazaar: India, Morocco, Syria.
Includes index.
ISBN 978 1 74196 076 1 (pbk.)
1. Indian cookery. 2. Cookery, Moroccan. 3. Cookery, Syrian. 4. India – Social life and customs. 5. Morocco – Social life and customs. 6. Syria – Social life and customs.
I. Title.

641.595

Printed by 1010 Printing International Ltd in 2008
PRINTED IN CHINA.

The Publisher would like to thank Simon Johnson for lending props for use in photography

IMPORTANT: Those who might be at risk from the effects of salmonella poisoning (the elderly, pregnant women, young children and those suffering from immune deficiency diseases) should consult their doctor with any concerns about eating raw eggs.

CONVERSION GUIDE: You may find cooking times vary depending on the oven you are using. For fan-forced ovens, as a general rule, set the oven temperature to 20°C (35°F) lower than indicated in the recipe. We have used 20 ml (4 teaspoon) tablespoons.